D1193245

Learning
to
Play
the
Game

My Journey through Silence

Jonathan **Kohlmeier**

ISBN: 978-1-4834-5912-7 (sc)
ISBN: 978-1-4834-5913-4 (e)

Library of Congress Control Number: 2016915990

Because of the dynamic nature of the Internet, any web addresses or links contained in this book may have changed since publication and may no longer be valid. The views expressed in this work are solely those of the author and do not necessarily reflect the views of the publisher, and the publisher hereby disclaims any responsibility for them.

Cover photo by AnaMaria Garcia

Lulu Publishing Services rev. date: 10/03/2016

Contents

Part 4
Quintessence of Dust

For you

Acknowledgments

I'd like to thank the following people, without whom I don't know where I'd be—or even *if* I'd be: my family, Dr. Kurtz, Dr. Bennett, Ms. Avecilla, Ms. Perez, Dr. Eisner, Ms. Eurell, Mr. Fyfe, Ms. Spira, Marsha, Dennis, Ana, Gemma, Aisling, Adam, Evan, Xizi, Lily, Lauren, and all the people who helped me along the way, even though sometimes they (and oftentimes I) didn't realize it.

Introduction

What Is *It*?

Imagine that every conversation in your life was like getting up on stage at the Met, naked, in front of three thousand people.

It is a feeling I get when I feel like I can't do something, when something bigger than me is standing in the way. Some people might be deathly afraid of spiders or snakes or heights. I'm deathly afraid of other people. Just think of your worst fear and having to live with it all the time—forever. The threshold of when I begin to feel *it* changed as I got older, but *it*'s the same feeling. I feel as though I'm constantly being watched. The problem is that I've come to like being with other people. That'd be like being afraid of spiders but having a tarantula as a pet, by choice. I know this must seem confusing, but I've lived with *it* for nineteen years, and even I don't understand *it*.

When I was younger, *it* was something that I just dealt with. When I felt *it*, I knew I was doing something with which I was uncomfortable. Eventually, I learned that *it* was supposed to be good. When I felt *it*, I was getting outside my comfort zone. And when I was even younger than that, most of the time I felt like I was sick or had a stomachache. When that happened, usually my parents or my doctor had to tell me what to do. Now that I'm older, *it* is very different. I still get those feelings of terror, when I feel like I can't do certain things, but nowadays, I know ahead of time when I'm going to have a problem. That'd be like being terrified of tarantulas but liking having one as a pet and purposely going to buy another one but still being deathly afraid.

Only recently have I found "*It* 2.0." It's kind of like movie reels spinning in my head about this thing and that thing that happened. The movies just keep going and going, faster and faster. Sometimes I can get stuck watching, and I know I need to stop, but

I don't know how. That's the most frustrating part. Getting angry and upset about the things that happened in the past, the stuff I missed out on, doesn't help. It still happens, though. Someone told me it's like getting stuck in quicksand. I've never been stuck in quicksand ... but it's something that you can't control, and when you try to control it, *it* gets worse. It gets to a point when nothing seems real, and I don't understand what's happening, and I get very confused. The frustration is the worst part because I'm so close to letting *it* go but so far from being able to do so.

It happens when I start to think about all those things I've missed out on so far and can never go back and change. That's when my head starts to spin. I know I'm being repetitive, but I'm trying to help you to understand something that I don't understand, and I'm living through the feelings, and they are repetitive.

I can remember times when I was little when it was just me and my mom somewhere in the house, and I was crying. Those were the bad days, usually when things became too much or something happened at school. On the really bad days, my mom would say to me, "Whenever you're ready to write a book, I'll be ready." So much happened and was happening. I'm not sure anything can make it worth it or even if it's worth thinking about. I don't know what it's like to not have this or to not think like this, but I think that it's different. It has to be. I wonder what normal feels like. This curiosity keeps me up at night and is almost as bad as *it*. It was easier when I didn't know what normal looked like.

When I was figuring out what I wanted to do for my senior project in high school, I eventually decided to write this book. As I grew older, I stopped talking to my mom about *it*. *It* had become something that we didn't bring up at home unless there was a problem. And even then, I would refuse to talk to her about *it*, even if she asked. I would just get mad and yell at her to stop.

I knew I needed to talk to her about wanting to write the book because I couldn't remember a lot of what happened when

I was little, but I felt a lot of memories. It took me two months from when I decided to write the book until I told her about my project. I walked into her bedroom one Saturday morning when my dad wasn't home. I sat in the chair in the corner of her room. She was changing the sheets on her bed. I asked her what she thought I should do for my project, hoping that she would think of the book. After five minutes of her offering suggestions about flying lessons or working on the stock market—and me getting frustrated with her for giving me "stupid" ideas—I told her that I'd already decided. I told her I wanted to write a book. I reminded her of what she used to say to me when I was little. She stopped what she was doing, looked at me, and replied, with a kind of smile on her face, "But I don't know if I'm ready."

"Well, too bad. Get ready," I said to her.

I knew that was a little mean, but I didn't want anything to stop me from doing this. I had more than enough in myself to stop me already.

I don't know what I think all about this. I'm not sure what I need to realize and know. Part of me thinks this is just life, and I just need to get over it because there is nothing I can do. The other part of me knows that isn't true, and there is something that I can do. I think I've been doing a lot. I don't think I would've made much progress if I wasn't doing anything. I wouldn't be the person I am today if *it* wasn't always there in the background. And I think I'm happy about the person I am. I don't know what else I'd want. If I could redo my life and was allowed to choose whether or not to have selective mutism and social anxiety, I don't think I would change anything. Everything's a lesson and a story. Life's about gathering stories.

I want to tell you—whoever you are—my story

Note: I have tried to make this book as true to memory as possible. I have changed the names of people and places for privacy reasons.

Part 1
Elementary School

Chapter 1
Where *It* All Began

The problem with the beginning of my story is that I was very young. I can't remember all of what happened. Some of this is because I was just too young to remember or understand what was happening. The other part is that I think my memory is hiding some of the stuff from me because it knows that I start to feel bad when I think about *it*...

My parents never really noticed a problem with me before I was in elementary school. According to my mom, I was friendlier than my older brother, Justin. When we were young, neither of us was very social. I would usually get bugged out by large crowds, but my parents never took much notice. They thought that I was just a shy kid. And that was okay. When I started preschool, I was still kind of shy, but it wasn't a problem. I only talked to the assistant teacher. A few times, the head teacher yelled at me for not responding, but I couldn't help it. I didn't think anything of it at the time. Everyone thought that I was a shy kid who was entering school for the first time and that I would warm up and outgrow it.

Well, that didn't happen.

I remember the first day of kindergarten as if it happened yesterday. The night before, I was so excited because I was starting elementary school with my brother, who was entering third grade. My mom knew that it might be hard for me, so she promised that we would go to McDonald's after school, and my brother got mad at her because she didn't tell him. I was so excited. I felt that raw excitement that people rarely experience after childhood. I could never have imagined what was going to happen.

That morning, I went to school on the bus with my brother. I started to get nervous. A lot of people get nervous when they do new things. This was just like that—but at the same time, nothing like that. My brother always made me feel calmer because he was there to protect me. I always stayed close to him, and he probably got used to it. He'd answer for me when people tried to talk to me. We got on the bus, and I sat with him. Because he was in third grade, I got to sit in the middle of the bus, while all of the other kindergarteners had to sit in the front. I followed him in but sat by the window. I loved the window seat because I could look outside and pretend I wasn't there. I'd pretend to be the people I saw outside of the bus. A lot of times, I counted the houses or whatever else I could see to try to be somewhere else. We lived five minutes away from the school by car, which meant the bus picked us up last and dropped us off last on the way home.

When we got to school, I felt as if I were walking into a place where I knew I was going to die—painfully. That's how much I didn't want to go. When we got off the bus, I followed my brother to the building. There were too many kids to keep track of and to watch. I had to stop looking. I looked down at my feet and followed my brother. As soon as I saw the entrance to the building, I yanked on my brother's arm. A long cement hallway led from the street to the front door. All I could see was dark gray, damp cement. It felt like a dungeon, with a few openings for sunlight and air. Comically yet sadly, the hall seemed intentionally designed to look like a dungeon.

Finally, we reached the door and entered the building. The stark whitish-gray of the inside was almost blinding compared to the dungeon-like entrance. The building was separated into two wings with two floors each. The kindergartners were on the first floor, down the hall on the right side; my brother was on the first floor too but all the way down the hall on the left.

When we got to the middle of the main lobby, my brother had to go down his hall. He saw kids he knew and was talking to them. I silently screamed-whispered his name a few times, but he had to go. He told me he would see me later and left. I, along with other little kids, was sent down the opposite hallway to our classrooms. Our wing was separated from the rest of the school by two wooden double-doors, another barrier trying to keep me inside. As the doors closed, they swung the opposite way, as if tempting me to go back or to leave a small opening to escape, but the weight of the doors eventually stopped them from swinging, and they shut with a thump.

My classroom was way down the hall on the left side. My teacher's name was Ms. Jackson. She seemed young; she was tall and had brown hair. A few weeks before school started, my mom and I had come to the school to talk to the principal to figure out which teacher and class would be good for me. School administrators did this for all the kindergarteners. I knew kids from the neighborhood and from the preschool I went to. They wanted to make sure it'd be a good fit.

I walked slowly toward the classroom door, but once at the door, I only took one step inside the classroom. I just stood by the door. No matter what the teacher did, I wouldn't move from that spot, directly to the left of the door under the light switch. I can't remember much that happened after that. I just know that's where I stood for the entire time we were in class. If my class went to another room or to lunch, I would follow them, but I didn't go into any of those rooms either. I stood by the door like a Secret Service agent monitoring what was happening in the room. Occasionally, I looked over my shoulder outside the room, but for the most part, I just stared at the class.

For a long while, I never sat down, ate, talked, or used the bathroom in school. When people talked to me, I shook my head yes or no and shrugged my shoulders to indicate "I don't know." (You'd be surprised how far those three gestures can get you.) Teachers became angry with me and called the principal in, but none of them was able to get me to do anything. The other kids stared at me too.

On that first day, the school called my mom at work around 10:30. She was in a caseworker meeting and was called out to answer the call from school. They just wanted to let her know that I was standing one step inside the classroom by the light switch. What was she supposed to say to them? They told her that they'd deal with it. And that was that.

This went on for weeks. When I came home from school, my mom asked how school was, and I didn't say anything. I had nothing to say about it. If she asked specifically, I told her about my teacher and the kids in class but never about anything else. My behavior was probably as much of a shock to me as it was to her. We both knew that we each knew what had happened. For a while, when I got home from school, I would go to my room, close the door, and cry. I cried until I was done and ready to come out of my room. My mom eventually understood that it was my way of "cooling down." She just needed to leave me alone until I was finished.

Turns out, I have no memory of this. When I was seventeen, I asked my mom about when I was little. I knew that I'd had frequent meltdowns, but I had no idea that it was every day after school for an hour or two at a time.

A week later, the school called my mom again to meet with the principal and school psychologist. The date was September 11, 2001. The school principal, Mr. Anderson, said I wasn't "adjusting" to elementary school. The school psychologist, Dr. Taylor, tried to explain to my mom that I had "severe anxiety issues," and I needed to be transferred to a school in the district that focused on "therapeutic rehabilitation," where they would know how to deal with me. They told my mom that I was going to be this way for the rest of my life and that she needed to understand this. They were nasty about the whole thing too, as if Mom and I purposely wanted to give them a hard time.

During the meeting, Mr. Anderson and Dr. Taylor asked my mom if I had suffered any traumatic events that would explain my behavior. My mom said no. They asked about any surgeries I'd had or doctors I had seen recently. A year before, I'd had my tonsils taken out, but I was fine after I recovered. I went back to preschool a week later. The principal was convinced that my not speaking was caused by this traumatic event. My mom was convinced that they didn't know what they were talking about and that they didn't know me.

Earlier that year, when I was still in preschool, the principal had recommended to my parents that I see a psychologist. I went to a preschool with only ten kids in my class. It was at a nearby temple, Temple Beth Shalom. I didn't have many issues there. I did everything they asked me to do. My mom never had a problem getting me out of the car or going in, nor was she called to pick me up early because I wanted to leave. I just didn't talk, eat, or go to the bathroom while I was at preschool. They just thought I was really shy. The assistant teacher was very nice to me. I talked to her a few times, but the head teacher was a "fucking bitch," according to my mom. She told my parents that I had an anxiety issue, but she also told my mom not to feed me. The head teacher believed that I knew what I was doing and needed to be punished. She said that the reason I wasn't eating at school was because my mom had food for me when I got home. Because I always wore the same clothes to preschool, the teacher also was convinced that my mother was neglecting me. This teacher didn't know that finding clothes that I felt comfortable in was hard. When we did find a shirt or a pair of pants, we bought ten of the same thing. In preschool, I only wanted to wear black or navy blue cotton T-shirts and sweatpants.

In the spring of preschool, I started to see Dr. Roberts, a child psychologist who also happened to, ironically, be deaf. He too told my parents that they shouldn't feed me. He said they needed to take things away from me and be very strict because I was being oppositional. I saw him only three or four times before we never went back. After that, it was summer, and I stopped seeing a psychologist. My parents couldn't stand him. I can't remember any of it.

My mom told this to the people at my new elementary school during the meeting, but the conversation was interrupted when the principal's wife called, saying, "Something's happening. I see smoke from the buildings." He replied, "Not again." He told my mom that they lived in lower Manhattan, and they must be doing work on the World Trade Center. They ended the meeting when the chaos began. They planned to reschedule, but with what had just happened, the next meeting didn't take place for another three weeks. Another three weeks of my standing by the light switch and meltdowns when I came home. A lot happened during those weeks, though.

A close family friend, Vincent, was killed in one of the buildings. So were a lot of other people, friends, mothers, fathers, and children.

We pretty much lost the month of September because of what happened. Vincent was my dad's best friend. My dad wasn't up for much of anything. He went over to Vincent's house to see his wife, Julie, and their three kids. He took out their garbage and helped however he could. He started a fund for them and raised over one hundred thousand dollars. He is a financial advisor, so he was good at that kind of stuff. They came over to our house a lot, and we went over to theirs too.

At the next school meeting, nothing had changed with me. The principal continued to push my mom to send me to the special school, but my parents kept refusing. The school psychologist recommended another doctor for me. His name was Dr. Wilson, and he was a children's play therapist. We played board games together in his office. At first, my mom played too, but once I became comfortable with him, he and I played alone. After a few sessions, he managed to get me talking, but there were still no changes at school. I wasn't getting better. I didn't want to go to school. I went to the nurse almost every day. The school called my mom a lot to pick me up.

It felt like no one knew what they were doing. Yellow brick roads don't exist in real life—there's no path to follow to end up in the right place. There were no directions or rules to follow. We had to learn new rules as we went.

In the first month of kindergarten, the school had a fire drill. I heard the alarm screech above my head. I didn't panic. I followed the teacher outside. The class walked to the parking lot behind a row of trees. I was standing in line, just looking around. I was always great at fire drills because the teachers always yelled at kids to stop talking. I never talked, so I was fine. I saw my teacher looking at the rest of the kids, counting them and smiling. When she got to me, her smile faded. She frowned at me dramatically. I think it was her way of showing disapproval of how I was acting. My heart sank. I didn't know what I'd done. She just stared at me for a few seconds and then went back to smiling and looking around. I just wanted to hide and become invisible.

The rest of that day went along just like all the others, with me standing by the door. Of course, months later, after a doctor explained everything to her, she became one of the nicest people in the school to me. But that's how it went with most of the teachers there.

In my classroom, a small poster hung above the blackboard. It read "Treat others how you would like to be treated." I always laughed when I saw the sign because I knew that the teachers were the ones not following its message. I knew that if you were afraid to speak, you wouldn't want someone yelling at you about not listening and following directions. I knew it was just because they didn't understand, but that still made the sign funny.

Everyone just automatically assumed they knew everything about me. But the truth is that no one really *knows* anything about anyone. The only real thing to know is that we know nothing.

Chapter 2

Drifter

Just before Thanksgiving break, my class had a party, and we colored turkey placemats and did other kindergartener stuff. My mom came to school later that day, the first time she was in class with me. I knew she was coming and was pretty excited about it before she got there.

When she came in, she saw me standing by the door. She stood there with me. I slowly moved farther down the wall away from her and the door and moved behind a bookcase that was like an island near that side of the room. My excitement vanished as more parents came into the room. I wanted to be invisible. As the kids and parents worked on their projects, I calmed down enough to sit on the floor next to my mom to make a placemat. She tried to get me to sit at my desk, which had remained empty since the beginning of the year. I didn't respond or even acknowledge her. When we finished, she tried to show the teacher, but I angrily pulled it away and shook my head. I saw in her face that she was upset, trying to not cry in front of me. When she left, she was surprised that I didn't grab on to her or beg her to take me home. It wasn't about wanting to be with her or wanting to go home. It was just too hard to get in there and be present.

Principal Anderson and Dr. Taylor called my mom in later and said, "Mrs. Kohlmeier, you need to understand this is who your son is, and you need to come to terms with it. He will never be anything different than what he is now." She got really angry at them. She wanted to smack them both. She left the office crying. My mom said she would never forget what they said to her that day.

The school kind of gave up after that. The principal told my teachers to let me do whatever I wanted and to leave me alone, and they did. The principal was waiting for my mom to let them send me to the other school. They didn't really bother with her or me anymore. I just stood by the door.

My mom kept refusing to send me to the other school. She spoke to friends who knew me and who knew the school district. They all told her to not let them send me to that school. They said if I went to the other school, I would stay the same. They all knew me as a normal kid at home. I spoke to them, yelled, and played with their kids. No one understood what was going on. I had been over to other kids' houses from school. I was pretty social with the kids I knew and liked.

In December, my mom was tired of the lack of progress with my therapist, Dr. Wilson. The school psychologist, Dr. Taylor, recommended that I see a psychiatrist in town. The new doctor's practice was oddly located in the basement of his house. He evaluated me and diagnosed me with generalized anxiety disorder, oppositional defiance disorder, and maybe a form of high-functioning autism. My mom thought the guy was crazy. She knew her son wasn't defiant. He believed I knew what I was doing and was doing it on purpose. My mom spoke to two of her friends, one of whom was a clinical social worker. The other was an assistant principal at another school. They both told her that the doctor was crazy and his diagnosis wasn't me. We never went back to him. Thankfully.

After that we continued to see Dr. Wilson because my mom didn't know what else to do. But something funny happened in January. Dr. Wilson needed emergency surgery, and he lost his voice. He couldn't speak at all. First, a deaf doctor and now, a doctor who couldn't speak.

As expected, my mom became frantic. She continued to look for other doctors and asked friends if they knew anyone. Julie told my mom that one of Vincent's friends was the director of

Empire State University's Child Study Center. Julie said she would ask the director to contact my mom.

She also spoke to two other friends, a couple whose son had a phobia of the outdoors and bugs. Sometimes, he wouldn't go outside. They talked to my mom about the school district and about laws my mom didn't know about, such as that the school couldn't force me to go to the special school and that I didn't need to "pass" kindergarten to move up to first grade. The school couldn't do anything without her permission. Also, they couldn't expel or suspend me, because I wasn't doing anything wrong. I always did my work at home, and I showed up for school. Another friend who also lived down the block had a son with other phobia issues. Both kids saw a doctor named Dr. Adler, who was from a town nearby.

My mom also reached out to a pediatrician who lived a few houses down, and he gave her the names of four psychologists. One had a kid in the same school, so he couldn't work with me. Another had a full schedule, and the other two didn't call her back. By this time, though, my mom finally was given an appointment at the Child Study Center at Empire State University in New York City, thanks to Julie. The drive took an hour and a half, but she was willing to do anything.

I met with a lot of different doctors, and so did my parents. ESU did many assessments on me and asked every possible question about me, my family, and our living situation. Because I didn't talk to them, I pointed to different smiley faces, depending on the anxiety I was experiencing. After they did all the tests, which lasted the entire day, we went home. Around the same time, my mom reached out to Dr. Adler, who worked at ESU, but she didn't know that yet.

Later that week at the weekly case meeting, when all the doctors learned about the new cases for the week, they diagnosed me with the anxiety disorder known as selective mutism—a childhood anxiety disorder characterized by a child's inability to speak in certain social settings. A doctor at ESU specialized in these cases, but Dr. Adler volunteered to take my case. At the time, he specialized in ADHD and phobias, but after hearing my story, he was fascinated by how I just stood by the light switch at school from September until March. He also lived nearby, which was much more convenient, because some of the treatment needed to be at school. They let him take the case under the supervision of the other doctor, who was the specialist. They hadn't reached out to my parents yet.

At the same time, my mom's friend, who was an assistant principle in New York City, was at a conference on mental health issues in children. She just so happened to pick up information about this new diagnosis called selective mutism. She immediately called my mom and said, "This is Jon." She read to my mom from the article. Afterward, my mom said, "Oh my God, this is my son." Selective mutism was a brand-new diagnosis, based on a doctor's research at Harvard. There wasn't much information out about it—at least not information that was reliable.

Later that week, after dinner one night, my mom sat at the kitchen table, staring out through the French doors that led to our back deck. My brother and I were in the back room, watching TV. My mom remembers that at the time, my brother and I "were still friends," and I "didn't hate him yet." My dad was out at a meeting, one of his two nights a week my mom allowed him to not be home for dinner.

My mom was really upset. She was tired. She was thinking about the pain I was going through, and she couldn't figure out how to help me. She felt like she was being beaten up every day by various people who told her different things about what was best for her son. Everyone had an opinion. She was doing all she could, but nothing was helping. She didn't think she was doing the wrong thing, but she couldn't accept what the school was telling her: that I'd never get better. My mom's parents lived downstairs from us, and they saw a lot of what was happening, especially my grandfather, who didn't work. My grandmother told my mom to let me stay home, that she was "torturing" me. My grandfather tried to support my mom's decisions. When she dropped me off at school on the bad days, she would call him and cry.

That night, while she was sitting at the table, crying and thinking about what to do next, the phone rang. She wasn't in the mood to pick it up, and she didn't recognize the number on the caller ID. She thought that maybe it was one of the doctors, even though it was late. She pulled herself together enough to answer the phone.

The caller said, "Hi, this is Dr. Adler." He had just left work for the day and was on the train back home. "I've heard about this little boy who stands by the light switch, and I need to meet him.

My mom told him about the school's diagnoses and that they wanted to send me to a different school. He told her not to worry. All she could do was cry on the phone, but this was a different cry. She felt like she was finally talking to someone who knew what to do and who wasn't going to give up on me, unlike all the other doctors.

My mom immediately made an appointment to see him that week at his office. The first appointment was for my mom and dad. He explained to them the process, what he would do, and that they needed to be involved, as did the school. My parents weren't sure how the school would react to the doctor's coming into the school to work with me during the day.

After Dr. Adler met with my parents, I began treatment after school at his ESU office and, later, at his office near my house. I didn't think much about it at the time. I had been to a few doctors by this time, and he was just another one. Therapy would start with my mom and me playing or talking in a room, and he would gradually move in and out of the room, depending on how I responded—either shutting down or continuing to be myself. Eventually, the plan was that I would become comfortable enough to talk to my mom with him in the room, and then I would begin talking to him too. The hope was that once I realized nothing bad was going to happen with him there, it would be easier for me. It was all based on gradual change to adapt my body and to realize the overreaction. It's called "exposure therapy," and it was the way I learned to deal with *it*. When I did things out of my comfort zone that I normally wouldn't do, I received "Brave Bucks" as a reward. They were pieces of red paper that looked like fake money, except there was a cartoon picture of Batman on the front. Once I earned enough Brave Bucks from "Brave Talking," I would get a prize, usually a toy for my hamster. It worked amazingly well. I was remarkably excited to earn these pieces of red paper.

In the middle of April, while I was still working with Dr. Adler in his office, the school held a Committee on Special Education meeting about me to talk about the rest of the year and plans for next year. My mom remembers the meeting vividly because it was the first time someone in the district gave a fuck about what was happening. Principal Anderson, Dr. Taylor, a teacher from school, a parent advocate, Dr. Adler, my parents, and Dr. Rossi, who was the assistant chairperson on the Committee on Special Education for the district, were all at the meeting. The first thing they did was review my case, and then the school told my parents that I didn't belong there because I had such-and-such problems.

This time, however, Dr. Adler basically told them they were idiots and weren't trying to help. As Dr. Adler explained selective mutism (SM) to them, Dr. Rossi told his assistant to get some books from his office, which he then gave to my parents. When Dr. Adler was finished, Dr. Rossi began interrogating the staff about the different assessments they were supposed to have completed. He then yelled at them, telling them they hadn't done what they were supposed to do for "this child." They were probably embarrassed and might have felt guilty at this point. Turns out that someone in Dr. Rossi's family happened to have SM. He knew all about it.

He ordered them to let Dr. Adler do whatever he needed to help me in school and to not interfere.

Principal Anderson and Dr. Taylor both ended up retiring at the end of the year. We all were very glad about that.

Dr. Adler came to school with me twice a week, sometimes with my mom, sometimes not. He got permission for me to be excused from some of the special classes, like art, music, and gym. We did work in the classroom while the other kids were at the specials and the room was empty. He taught the psychology intern what to do, and I worked with her almost every day. At first, my mom had to help a lot. But as I became more comfortable working with Dr. Adler and realized he was helping me, I was able to work with him without needing my mom there.

They started by getting me to move farther into the classroom, past the light switch. My desk was the closest desk to the door, only a few feet from the light switch, but I still didn't want to sit there. They enticed me with Brave Bucks and other rewards. They sat there, hoping that I would copy them. Eight months after school began, I finally sat at my desk—one of the first times I'd sat down anywhere in school. We began my sitting down with the morning work that I didn't do by myself. They asked me questions: "What's your favorite color?" or "Can you give me the red crayon?" I responded, but I never engaged in conversation. This took a few weeks, but it worked—gradually.

At the end of May, Dr. Adler told my mom he was trying to get me to sit on the carpet on the other side of the room. I hadn't been anywhere in the classroom except for at my desk. The carpet seemed miles from the door. He told my mom to brace herself; he knew I was going to freak out. He planned to lift me up, bring me over to the carpet, and hold me there until I calmed down. Before he did all this, he told me what he was going to do. As usual, I refused, but when you are five, you don't have a choice when someone decides to lift you up.

***

From My Mom

It is a beautiful May morning, the type of spring day that you want to last forever. The sun is shining; birds are chirping. Today is the day we have planned for several weeks. I try to remember everything Dr. Adler said to me to stay calm—it'll be difficult. Jon will feel like the ground is opening up and swallowing him whole. I need to stay calm.

I get up early to get ready so as to avoid any mishaps.

I say, "Good morning, guys. Time to get ready for school." We are in a good routine by now; both boys get ready while I prepare breakfast: French toast sticks, their favorite. Justin comes out to the kitchen to eat. We have learned it is better for Jon when he eats in his room. It keeps him calm and avoids any potential brotherly love interactions in the morning.

"Jon, I am coming in with your breakfast," I say at the door. Jon is sitting on his bed watching one of his favorite shows. This seems to calm him and prepare him for the day. He's already picked out his favorite tie-dye T-shirt and navy blue sweatpants, a uniform for him now. I leave his breakfast on his desk.

By now, Jon knows what numbers to look at on the cable box to know when it's time to go. I am learning the fine line between encouraging him and increasing his anxiety.

It's time to go. Jon gets his backpack on and is ready. He knows that Dr. Adler and I will be meeting him at school today, a regular occurrence now. We have arranged for Jon to stay back when his class leaves to go to one of the "specials" periods. This helps to slowly desensitize Jon to the classroom and has been working so far. He will sit at his seat, in the first chair at the first table, only a few small steps into the classroom.

I try hard to calm my anxiety, butterflies in my stomach, and racing thoughts. I tell myself to stay calm and breathe deep. If Jon senses I am nervous, he will react to it. I keep reminding myself this is necessary, that this is an important step.

They are off to school. I sit and wait for 9:30, watching the clock, tick-tock, tick-tock. This is making me crazy, and I need to distract myself.

I go see my father, who is making himself breakfast.

"Hi, Daddy. How are you?"

He says, "What's up, Daddy? [My dad calls all his children *Daddy*.] Not going to work today?"

"Going in late," I tell him. "I need to go to school to meet Dr. Adler and Jon." I try not to tell him too much. I don't really want to think about what is going to happen, so we talk about tennis, the Australian Open, the upcoming French Open, and the Yankees.

It's time for me to go. Driving to the school only takes a few minutes. Breathe, just breathe. Stay calm. This is my mantra as I drive. I pull into the parking lot and see Dr. Adler waiting. I was half hoping he'd forget or have an emergency. But no, this is really going to happen today. I say, "Hi, Dr. Adler. How are you?"

"I'm good. How are you doing? Are you ready for today?" he asks.

"Ready as I'll ever be." We walk into the building. I have walked into this building hundreds of times before today, but today it feels different: I walk in with a sense of purpose, with a sense that today has the potential to be a pivotal day, a day that will be hard but worth it.

Jon's class is getting ready to leave for music. We wait patiently until Jon is the only one left in the room. He is sitting at his desk.

Dr. Adler begins. "Hi, Jon."

Jon speaks in a low voice. "Hi."

"Jon," Dr. Adler says, "today we are going to practice going to the carpet."

Jon's whole body immediately begins to tense up. He shakes his head no repeatedly, left to right, left to right.

"Jon, it will be hard, but your mom and I are here to help you. Remember how hard it was to sit in your seat and now you can come in and sit down? It will be the same thing—hard at first and then gradually easier." Jon shakes his head no again. Dr. Adler looks at me to let me know it is time.

Sweaty palms, stomach in a knot, I tell myself to breathe, just breathe. Stay calm.

Gently, Dr. Adler leans over Jon, picks him up, and carries him to the carpet. Jon begins to shake, trying to get out of his grasp and quietly saying, "No. No. No." The walk to the carpet is only a few paces, but it feels like miles.

Jon is on the carpet, feet planted on the floor, back to the wall. He is crying, now sobbing. His entire body is shaking. Dr. Adler stands in front of him. I am at his side. We are making a cocoon around him, partly to help him feel safe, partly to prevent him from running.

"Breathe, Jon," Dr. Adler says. "Breathe. It is okay. It is okay. All will be okay." Seconds feel like minutes, minutes feel like hours. *When will it be over?* I wonder. *When will this wave of emotion fade?*

Jon's breathing slows down. The sobbing returns to crying and then stops. The shaking stops. Jon has a shocked look on his face.

"See, Jon? You did it," Dr. Adler says quietly. "You are on the carpet."

Slowly, a smile comes on Jon's face, and his shoulders relax. He slides down the wall into a sitting position.

Finally, I can really breathe. Jon looks so comfortable. We all sit for a while, experiencing being in the space. I look up at the clock. It's almost time for the class to return.

Dr. Adler says, "Come on, Jon. Let's go back to your desk." Jon slowly rises with a tiny air of confidence and walks back to his desk.

I give Jon the routine. "Bye, Jon. See you later."

Dr. Adler stays until the teacher returns. Jon's classmates are used to seeing Dr. Adler in the classroom.

I am waiting for Dr. Adler outside of the school, working to contain my emotions.

Dr. Adler comes out. "Well, we did it. Jon did great. This is one of many hard experiences that will be worth it."

"I didn't realize how difficult it would be to contain my emotions," I tell him.

"Remember," he says, "it is very important to be as calm as possible when dealing with Jon. He can and will react to your anxiety. When he gets home, just act like it was a regular day."

"Okay," I respond. As I close the car door, my heart begins to pound. My hands are sweaty. I feel a rush of emotion, and the tears run down my face.

* * *

That day, with my mom in the classroom, Dr. Adler and I warmed up by getting me to sit at my desk. After a few minutes of my being calm, he told me what was going to happen. I started crying. I don't know why I was so scared. He picked me up out of my seat and brought me over to the carpet. He put me down in the middle of the carpet and held on to me. I was crying hysterically and shaking. If we'd been anywhere else, I probably would've yelled and screamed, but at school that would've made *it* worse. My mom had to turn away. She was crying. She said it looked like I felt I was being burned alive.

After a few minutes, which probably felt like an eternity to each of us, I stopped shaking and crying. I looked around and realized that nothing had happened. My mom came onto the carpet, and we read a book together.

Dr. Adler made a deal with me that if I was able to sit on the carpet, he would go right home to get his pet snake and bring it to my class for all the kids to see. When I reluctantly kept my end of the deal, he kept his. He drove home right after the other kids came back with my teacher. All the kids were so excited to see the snake. It was really thin and couldn't hurt anyone. The best part was that the snake shit on him while he was showing it to people.

Soon after, I began sitting at my desk during class. I did some of my work in school, but not all of it. I didn't like going to the different centers around the classroom for activities. I stayed in my chair, which was, I realized, better than standing at the door. I still earned Brave Bucks for everything I did—now, the teachers and the intern also gave them to me. My teacher, Ms. Jackson, and Ms. Murphy, my brother's teacher, arranged it so that our classes would be reading buddies. Once a week, my brother's class came to our class to read books to us. My brother was my reading buddy. At the time, he was the only kid I would interact with in school.

Slowly, the other kids began interacting with me too. I didn't talk back to them, but I smiled and laughed silently. They were very protective of me. They'd say to Dr. Adler, "He doesn't talk. Leave him alone," whenever he tried to get me to do something new. I went to birthday parties outside of school too. I would just stand and watch. Kids would play for a while and then come up to me to talk or make me laugh, and then they'd run back to playing. Things slowly started to get easier.

One of the last things that happened in kindergarten was when it was my turn to be "Kid of the Week." Each week one kid was allowed to do something special or do a show-and-tell. The last week of school was my week. My mom brought my hamster in to show my class. The other thing that happened was that Dr. Adler arranged to show a video he had taken the week before of me talking to him about my hamster. Unfortunately, I wasn't expecting it, and I became really angry. The kids were shocked when they heard me talking on the video. A lot of them thought that I truly couldn't speak. I freaked out when I saw their reactions. My dad tried to stop me from running out of the room, but I punched him in the stomach and ran out.

Dr. Adler ran outside and found me just outside the door. He calmed me down and brought me back inside. After the video, my mom talked about the hamster and how we took care of him. He was a Russian dwarf hamster. The kids then came up, one by one, to pet him. He was pretty friendly and never bit anyone, unlike some of the other hamsters I'd had when growing up. My mom remembers that I liked it and had a good time. This was the first time I interacted with most of my class and the first time in school with any of them.

Kindergarten ended substantially better than where it had begun. It was still horrendously difficult sometimes, but at least I was able to be there. There were still a lot of things I couldn't do. I still wore only my blue or black or sometimes tie-dye T-shirts with gray, blue, or navy sweatpants, even if it was warm out and most kids were wearing shorts.

Dr. Adler had me meet my first-grade teacher, Ms. Hill, before I left for the summer. I also went in a few times during the summer to try to get comfortable with her. I visited my classroom and picked out my seat. I picked the seat closest to the door, like in kindergarten. Ms. Hill's class was laid out almost the same as my kindergarten class, but it wasn't as far down the hall. And all the kids' chairs had yellow tennis balls at the end of the legs so they wouldn't squeak horrendously when they were pushed around.

Chapter 3

Cold Water

The summer after kindergarten I began going to day camp. My parents wanted to get me out of the house, meet other kids, and make sure I didn't get too comfortable away from people. We knew I had to go to camp because if I stayed home with my grandfather, I'd have never wanted to leave the house when it came time for school in September. Dr. Adler told my parents that they should send me to camp and my parents listened to 98 percent of what Dr. Adler told them anyway. That meant, I had to go to camp.

Before summer began, my parents spoke to the owners of the camp about my "situation." The owners were an older couple and very nice. They said to my parents, "If you're fine with paying for him to come here and all he does is sit under a tree, it's fine with us." The hope was that I wouldn't just sit under a tree all day, but even if I did, it would be better than me staying at home all day all summer.

Dr. Adler and my parents came with me to walk around the camp to get the lay of the land so I might feel better about it. We met my counselors beforehand. Dr. Adler talked to them about how they should push me but also leave me alone when I wasn't in the mood. We came up with the plan that if I needed anything, I would raise my right index finger in the air. Because I wouldn't talk to them, they knew they'd need to get my brother if I did raise my finger. Most of the time, it was just to get a drink. When my group was in the cafeteria, and I raised my finger, they would find my brother. He would get a cup of pink lemonade and come with me into one of the bathroom stalls so I could drink it. The counselors and especially my mom were always worried I was going to become dehydrated and pass out. I never ate lunch there.

Later on, when I was older, I would sometimes take an ice cream at the end of the day, but that was usually only when I felt like death was imminent.

I didn't sit under a tree all day, but I also didn't do most of the activities. I didn't do any of the team sports or swimming. I played catch with a tennis ball with my counselors once in a while, but that was usually when I sat to the side as the other kids in my group were doing something else. I sometimes did ceramics, but my absolute favorite activity was archery. Every free chance, I wanted to go to the archery fields. I liked it so much because I was really good at it. And my brother did it too. Only about four of us at camp liked it and were good at it. We even competed with one another. When I was older, my parents gave me my own bow to use at camp. They also bought a target to use at home. We practiced in the backyard. I loved putting the arrow in the bow, pulling it back, and focusing on the target. It was just me, the bow, and the target. Nothing else mattered in those few seconds. I loved hearing the slap of the arrow hitting the target.

I was so proud of it too. I told Dr. Adler all about it, and he came to see me. My parents and grandparents came to watch during open house. The older woman who was teaching me told my parents that my brother and I should keep it up because one day we could go to the Olympics. I'm pretty sure she was just being nice and trying to make my family feel good. We didn't stay with it when we got older.

Swimming was the worst part of camp. I wasn't going to take my shirt off to go swimming, and I definitely wasn't going to change with all the other boys in my group. I was born with some problem with my rib cage, where it looks like there is a big dent in the middle of my chest. That didn't help *it* at all. The doctors thought of fixing it when I was little, but they would've had to take my rib cage out of my chest to fix it. My parents agreed it wasn't worth the risk as long as it didn't give me any health problems.

The pool area had four rectangular pools and was always chaotic. Too many little kids ran around making much too much noise. I didn't follow the no-shoes rule in the pool area either. I just sat on bleachers by the side of the pool and watched. Sometimes I counted the kids or counted the colors they were wearing—anything to make time go by.

We had a pool at home. Incidentally, my mom really wanted me to learn to swim, so she had the camp lifeguards run private swimming lessons for me after camp, when only a few people were around. I still wouldn't go in. They couldn't get me to change into a bathing suit or even stick my feet in the water. But every day for five weeks, I went after camp to swimming lessons with this one woman. Sometimes my mom came to help if she could but not all the time.

One day, after all the other kids went home, I walked into the kiddy pool with all my clothes on, even my shoes. I can't remember why I finally did it that day, but I walked down the little ramp halfway into the pool. The pool wasn't deep, and I walked from the one end, as it gradually became deeper, like at the beach, to the other end. The swimming teacher and my mom didn't care that I went in with my clothes on; at least I was in the water. After five weeks, I'd finally done it. I only stayed in for a few seconds. I walked back out, and we went right home. My mom put purple towels on the seats so I wouldn't get the car all wet.

Later on, I began finding "my people"—those with whom I was comfortable. Jamie, my brother's camp counselor, brought him to me whenever I needed something. I started to really like her. I eventually began asking for her when things became too much. One day, one of my counselors tried to get me to go into the camp's little water park and to a big red-and-yellow mushroom with water falling down the sides. She kept asking me if I wanted to go in, and I kept shaking my head no.

Before I knew it, she came up from behind me, picked me up, and tried to run with me into the fountain. I tried to get away, but I couldn't. I was soaked with all my clothes on, and it was still a while until the day would be over. I was so mad at her. She brought me back to the same spot where I'd been standing. I started crying uncontrollably. One of the other counselors ran to get Jamie, and she came over from the office in a golf cart. She shot a glare at the other counselor and brought me back to the main office. My mom came to get me. I never saw the counselor who grabbed me again. Jamie began babysitting for us. She also gave me swimming lessons at home. She knew how to deal with me.

Even though I eventually kind of found my place at camp, my favorite part of the day was the bus ride home. The minibus was air-conditioned. I was fine with going on the bus because there were so few people: the bus driver, a counselor, and three to five kids, depending on the day. Most of them stayed quiet, and I often fell asleep on the bus. Sometimes, this one girl wouldn't shut up. She just wouldn't stop talking and bothering people. I tried to ignore her.

One day in particular, for some random reason, we had a party on the bus. The counselor brought popcorn and chips. On the bus, the girl kept trying to talk to me. I didn't respond and stared out the window, as usual. After a while, she started throwing popcorn at me. The first few times she missed, but then she started hitting me in the head. She kept laughing and throwing popcorn. The counselor and another kid told her to stop, but she didn't. No one seemed to be doing anything. I got up and ran over to her seat, which was two rows behind me. As she was still laughing, I put both my hands around her neck and started strangling her. She started gasping and turning red. The counselor and the other kids were yelling at me to stop, but nothing worked. Everyone was shocked, especially me. Another kid yanked me off her. I ran back to my seat, started crying, and stared out the window. She never bothered me again, though. I don't understand why the camp didn't kick me out or at least off the bus. My mom was called in, and they talked to her, but nothing happened.

After a few years at day camp, my brother became really interested in cooking, so he started going to a chef camp nearby. I went with him, partly because I didn't want to be at camp by myself and partly because it was indoors and air conditioned.

Chapter 4

The Lion's Den

During the summer, my mom drove past the school with me as often as she could. Once in a while we went to the school's playground to play or to see some events on the school's fields. I needed to face my fear as often as I could because if I didn't, going back would've been that much worse. When things stay the same for too long, my progress can slowly drift away, and what used to be easy gets hard again. The same is still true for me today.

First grade was relatively uneventful because it was similar to kindergarten. That's probably why I had a lot of problems in second grade; with more expected of me, it became harder—like when the teachers wanted to see the work I did. For the first few years of school, my report cards said, "Progress could not be determined."

On my desk, I had a chart of assignments from Dr. Adler, things we'd agreed on previously. Doing different things awarded me different amounts of Brave Bucks. My teacher, Ms. Hill, always knew when to give them to me because before school began, Dr. Adler spoke with her; the new school psychologist, Dr. Allen; and the new psychology intern. I started going around the room to different centers during class.

On the days when my mom had trouble getting me into school, she would call Dr. Allen to say something like, "It's a bad day today." Dr. Allen always calmly replied, "Just get him in, and we'll take care of it," and then Dr. Allen would be waiting outside when we got there to take me in. Usually, I first went to her office, and we talked until I was ready to go to class.

I could whisper to Ms. Hill if I went up to her desk and no one was around. I also once whispered to Vanessa, my mom's friend's daughter, during one of our center times when we were making something with stickers. It was the first time I had spoken to another kid in school. And I did it by myself. I can't remember exactly what I said or why I said it, but one of the other five kids at the table said, "Why doesn't Jon talk?" Vanessa replied, "He talks to me." And I whispered in her ear, "I do talk." I became pretty good at whispering in such a way that no one else could hear besides the person I was talking to, or at least it seemed that way.

The younger kids were always let out of school first to get on the buses to go home so we wouldn't get trampled by the big kids. This was good for my brother because I was able to save him a good seat. He told me to sit toward the middle of the bus because he could sit with the rest of the older boys. I think in most schools, the older you are, the farther back you can sit on the bus. The older kids are territorial about the whole thing. I wonder who started this and how it spread to so many schools. Or if all kids have an animalistic territorial instinct when riding the bus. For me, it was "cool" to sit farther back in the bus. Once in a while, younger kids would test the limits of the system and sit one row farther back. Sometimes they were successful in their invasion, but rarely did the addition of territory last more than a day. Most of the time, the invaded would push the invaders out. The younger kids always listened when an older kid told them to move up.

I was always scared of sitting in the back of the bus because I thought the older kids would pick on me, but my brother asked me to save him his seat, and I would. He'd get mad at me for sitting too close to the front of the bus. He always sat with me nonetheless. He knew I needed him to protect me from the rest of the bus. He sat on the aisle, setting up a distinct division between everyone else and me.

One Tuesday morning, he told me to sit a little farther back on the way home, as if it were a tactic in territorial advancement for me to sit there first to save his spot. One of his friends must have said something to him about why he sat closer to the front.

Though the consequences rarely lead to anything noticeable, peer pressure in elementary school may be more intense, a bigger thing than when kids are older.

So that Tuesday at dismissal, they let us out of our classes and walked us to the buses. I knew which one was mine because they put a silver flag next to it, and it was usually the second to last bus in the row of buses. I got on the bus and sat a little farther than halfway down. My brother was in fourth grade and was allowed to sit behind the kindergartners, first-, second-, and third-graders. But he had to sit in front of the fifth-graders. Because I was his brother, I was allowed to sit there when he was there, and I was never there if he wasn't. Other kids began flowing in, grade by grade. Sometimes there were stragglers who didn't come out with their grade. For some reason, my brother was often one of them. At least, that's how it felt.

At first, when the third- and fourth-graders came on the bus, they didn't seem to notice me. But when the bus started filling up, and there were third-graders in front of me, they noticed a deer in the lion's den. One of the boys said, "What are you doing? You're not supposed to sit here." I didn't respond to him, but I felt sick to my stomach. I just sat there and continued looking out the window, waiting for my brother. He said, "Hey, kid?" I continued to ignore him, which probably made him angrier. He told the other kids I wouldn't move. Other kids then told me to move. Even a girl who was with them told me to move, which surprised me. After a few minutes, they said they were going to tell the bus driver. One of the kids started walking up the aisle. I grabbed my bag and ran to sit in an empty seat closer up.

I wasn't sure the bus driver even cared about the whole seating thing. Probably not. She just wanted everyone to be quiet and for no one to do anything they weren't supposed to do. I doubt she would have told me to move. I don't know what the kid said to the driver, but she came to the back, and one of the kids told her what happened. Because I wasn't there anymore, she didn't say anything and went back to her seat. I was so angry at them. Who the fuck cared where I sat? If it were a cartoon, steam would have been coming out of my ears. My brother finally got on the bus. He found me and sat next to me. He said, "I told you to sit farther back." In my yelling whisper, I said, "I did! They yelled at me to move!" and then I burst into tears. The kids in the back of the bus saw that my brother sat down with me, and I guess they realized who I was. The kid said to Justin, "Sorry, bro, we didn't know he was your brother." I shut down and wasn't there for the rest of the ride home. Most of the time when stuff like this happened, I wasn't really angry at the people but with what they had done. I think there is a huge difference.

If I've ever hated one person in my life, it was my elementary school gym teacher. The gym teacher raised her voice a lot—not just to me but to everyone. When I found out that she had three little sons, I couldn't believe it. The only way I was able to partly understand her yelling was to think that she must have thought I was a brat. I understood this in the beginning, but even after my parents, doctor, and other teachers spoke to her about it, it didn't get much better. Even after six years.

Eventually, she stopped yelling at me, but I don't think she understood why she should stop. I think she just didn't want to lose her job. Many times, the principal and the school psychologist had to talk to her. She wasn't alone. Before anyone knew I had a problem, everyone at school treated me like I was a difficult kid whose parents didn't know how to discipline their child.

When the class went to gym or any other special, I would be the first out the door but I would wait on the side until everyone else left the room. Then I would join the line at the back. I didn't want anyone walking behind me. If someone was, I could think of nothing else but the eyes of that person drilling into the back of my skull. I would aimlessly follow everyone else, robotically facing forward or looking toward the ground. I was always too worried about what was happening next. All I wanted was to be left alone. And that didn't happen often, which, in hindsight, may have been for the best.

Once in the gymnasium, I would always stand right next to the double doors. The gym was a gigantic rectangle encased in alternating dark green and light green foam mats fastened to the walls. The other kids had spots in alphabetical order along the wall across from the doors. Each dark green mat was a spot. I never went to my assigned spot. I could barely manage just being there, only five feet from the gym doors. A few mats farther from the door on the right, and I felt like I was being suffocated. At first, I couldn't even sit down. I stood by the door for the entire class. I was so scared of what would happen in gym class that my weekly time with the psychology intern was spent with her sitting next to me in gym class, preventing me from having a panic attack.

I eventually participated in one activity. We had "color war" once a year, when each class in the grade was put up against the other and earned points for winning. At the end of the week, the group that earned the most points was the winner. Once or twice I took part in tug-of-war. I would stand in the back and pull from the end. Everyone was just as surprised as I was. I was pretty good at it because I was a heavy kid. The only nice thing the gym teacher ever did was give extra points to our team whenever I participated. After it happened the first time, it was kind of like a standing deal.

In May, when the school was placing students in next year's classes, they decided that I would have Ms. Rosa for second grade. During the spring, my mom asked Ms. Rosa to come to our house once a week to tutor my brother, but it was really mostly for me so I would become comfortable seeing her. In school, Ms. Hill asked me to be her "messenger" a few times a week, when I would bring notes or nonsense things to Ms. Rosa.

At the end of the year during my CSE meeting, the Committee on Special Education wanted to take away some of the services they were providing me, like the psychologist and other help from the school. The woman running the meeting was adamant about it for some reason. She asked my mom, "Why do you think your son has improved so much?" My mom said, "Because treatment works, and if you take the services away, he won't be as successful." My mom ended up getting her way with the school district, as she had after the previous meeting.

Chapter 5

The Naughty List

In second grade, they realized that in addition to selective mutism, I also had social anxiety. They thought it might be a kind of performance anxiety. It became harder and harder for me to hand my work in to the teacher. I didn't want anyone to see it. I became really upset and frustrated with my handwriting. I never thought anything was good enough or finished. I couldn't do things quickly in class. I did not want to go into the building a lot. My mom needed to drive me in every day. In the car, the pain would be in slow motion, but time didn't move slower. No matter how much I tried, I wanted to pause time. I just needed to give myself a few minutes.

The teacher's assistant in my class would help me sometimes. We would go into the main office, and I would help her make copies. All copy rooms have this very distinct smell that is still calming to me today. Once I was ready, we would go back to class. Other times, I wouldn't go with her. Dr. Allen would bring me to her office. Once in a while, I would only come if my mom came, because she was my only way out of there. Eventually, Dr. Allen would tell my mom to leave, and she would close her office door on me. I sat in front of her door, crying, with my knees to my chest, watching my one possibility of salvation leave me. My mom wouldn't look back, even as she opened the door to go up the stairs. For some reason, and in some little remote place of me, I trusted Dr. Allen and my mom.

I was more frustrated with being trapped. One day in class, I picked up my chair and threw it across the room on the floor. I don't know what set it off but something made me overflow. Normally, when my frustration reached the top of the cup, the cup magically grew bigger. This time, it didn't. My usual apparent calmness and lack of external emotion was gone and then quickly appeared again. But throwing the chair made *it* worse because all the kids were looking at me. I ran up to my teacher and whisper-asked if I could go in the hall. She told me to stand in the doorway. After a few minutes, I couldn't take standing there anymore. So I left.

My teacher freaked out. They almost put the school in lockdown because they didn't know where I'd gone, which was to Dr. Allen's office. Dr. Allen didn't know I'd left without telling anyone. After she got it out of me, she called upstairs to let them know. After that, they realized I might need more help in school. I started going to the resource room, partly to help me feel more comfortable with my work but more to provide me a place to decompress during the day. It was a room for kids who needed more help academically. There was a teacher and a teaching assistant who helped the students with whatever we were struggling with. I went to help me with my writing but also so I could get away from my class for a little while. I went a few times a week. I looked forward to going because only five to ten kids were there at a time. And it was air conditioned. I also would go to the nurse during lunch to get away from the cafeteria. My mom sometimes came in during her lunch break to sit with me. We'd sit on the couch in the teacher's lounge.

I tried to run away from school a lot that year. I don't know why I was running or what was happening. All I remember is trying to run away. Trying to get far away. My mom used to call ahead to tell the school that there were "problems," and she would need help. The vice principal would be waiting when we got there.

One time when I was being dropped off at school, my mom walked me to my classroom at the end of the hallway. I really didn't want to stay, and I started crying and getting mad. She kept telling me to calm down, and after a few minutes, she knew that the only thing she could do was leave, even if I was in pain, screaming, and crying. I tried to run after her but the vice principal blocked me from getting to her. I kept trying to run toward my mom, even though he was holding me back. I was in a panic. I saw my mom look back at me, and she was crying. I saw her face. I didn't understand then, but I understand now. She was watching her child in a panic, and she knew she couldn't do anything about it. If she tried to help, she would only make it worse.

Recently, I took my dog to the vet because she cracked one of her nails, and the nail needed to be cut. I watched them put her on the table, and the nurse had to hold her down to help the doctor cut her nails. She was shaking and crying, as if someone were killing her. I felt sick. I can't imagine how my mom was feeling that day with me, considering this was just my dog, and I felt this horrible. I was my mom's own flesh and blood, screaming and crying for her.

After my mom turned and left, I collapsed on the floor, crying. After a minute or so, the vice principal brought me to my classroom. I watched other kids looking at me because I was crying, but it didn't matter. After a while, I finished crying, and that was the end of that. The rest of the day was just like every other.

The second time I tried to escape I wasn't even in the building yet. My mom drove me to school, as usual, in her white SUV. When we got there, I couldn't get out of the car. I sat there. She tried to get me out, but nothing she did worked. I can't remember exactly when it was, but I think it might have been in the fall during second grade. She called the same vice principal to come outside, and they both tried to get me out of the car. Somehow, they managed to do so, and then he grabbed me and tried dragging me into the building. I grabbed on to a tree near the car. I remember that the tree had almost no leaves left on it. He told my mom to drive away, and she did. I was still crying when she drove away.

My grip wasn't strong enough. His force made me let go of the tree, and he carried me into the building.

Later that year, during Christmas, my mom took me to buy presents for some of my teachers and people at school who'd helped me get through the tough times, even though I hated them a little for it. I can't remember where we went, but we found coal in a little red bag, kind of like a mini-version of Santa's sack, with two little yellow ends to close the bag. My mom thought it was perfect and hilarious. I agreed. The day before Christmas break, my mom and I went to the school's main office, and I gave it to the vice principal. You couldn't tell there was coal in the bag by looking at it. We laughed when he opened it. He knew there were times I hated him, but all those times were for the better, and he knew I knew that. And I kind of did know but not as much as I do now.

My parents thought one of the reasons I might be having problems in second grade was because we were doing construction on our house. For a while, we were living amid the construction. I didn't have my own room for three months. Once my mom realized how bad I was getting, she begged the contractor to finish my room first. I was the first to get my bedroom back. The house wasn't finished for another six months. There was always noise and too much going on. I hated all of it.

Chapter 6

Dynamite

In third grade I was tested to see if I had any academic issues because I became responsive enough to do the assessments. I took the usual IQ and processing tests. They didn't find any learning problems, indicating that my anxiety caused me to be slower in class. They provided me with extra time to do things. During the meeting after the tests, the head of the district asked Dr. Allen to redo the test because they didn't believe my 126 IQ result considering they thought I couldn't speak. She assured them it was accurate, and they left it alone.

Third grade was also the first time I ate lunch in school. My mom received permission to bring McDonald's for my class. The school essentially let her do anything for me at this point. She hoped it would get me eating in the cafeteria at our class table, but I ran out the door. My mom and I sat in the hallway. She brought my food from the cafeteria and tried to get me to eat. I eventually ate one French fry. The rest of the class ate in the cafeteria at our table, but it didn't matter that I didn't go in because it was still progress.

When I was eight, Dr. Adler brought up the idea to my parents of medicating me to help with my anxiety. He wasn't completely sure it would work, but he thought it might help. Some people thought that putting kids on antidepressant medication for anxiety helped with chemical imbalances. I don't know who thinks of these things, but I guess I'm grateful they did.

My mom was understandably scared about the whole idea. There were so many stereotypes and horror stories about medicating kids for mental "problems." When her brother was little, he was put on Ativan, which, on the dosage they put him on, made him a zombie. I was going to be put on a different type of medication, but they weren't sure of the side effects or the right dosage for kids. My mom did a lot of research, reading a lot of books and articles. She even went to a conference in New Orleans with the pediatrician who lived down the block from us. He asked my mom if she wanted to go with him so she could talk to professionals and get their opinions. She made sure that all the decisions she made for me were based on research and not what she or other people "believed" was right. One of the books she read was titled *Quirky Kids*.

The pediatrician thought the medicine could turn out to be a good thing. If I had imbalances with my heart, no one would've thought twice about giving me medicine. He didn't think this was any different. Doctors at the conference recommended I take Prozac, a selective serotonin reuptake inhibitor. I don't know exactly how it works, but it helps the brain better manage the chemicals that put me on threat detection DEFCON 1.

I started taking Prozac during the middle of third grade. The doctor started me on a small dosage. It took a few weeks for it to kick in, but when it did, I felt a lot better. It wasn't a magic pill, but it took a lot more for me to get to DEFCON 1. My mom remembers my telling her, "I don't feel so bunched up inside anymore." The medicine helped take down the walls that *it* tried to build up, brick by brick. I stayed on it for a few years and sometimes went back on it when too much was happening. I even went back on it when I went off to college because we got to the point where we could expect what was going to happen.

If you're wondering where my dad fit into the picture, he was always there in the background, supporting my mom when she needed it. He went to work first in the morning, but there were many times when my mom was so stressed out that she called him. He'd leave work to come back to the house. He was a little sterner with me about everything, which sometimes was what I needed. My parents made a good team. Somehow they were always on the same page. I don't remember them fighting about how to deal with me; I don't think they ever fought.

In kindergarten, when I first started having problems, my parents made a deal that my mom would be the one to make the decisions about school. My dad trusted her because she has three master's degrees: psychology, social work, and education. She was the "partner." He was the "junior partner." At first, these titles were a joke, but they really made the whole thing work. My mom was the one on the front lines, and my dad always supported her and me. They wanted to make life more manageable for me. My mom talked to my dad about what she was thinking, but she was the one to read the books and articles and talk to the doctors. My dad was very good at talking to the school and getting people to help me. He can be firm and persuasive to outsiders, so they give him what he wants.

By the end of third grade, I was practically like everyone else. No one could immediately notice a problem with me. We kind of got the recipe right by this time. I ate lunch in the cafeteria with everyone else, as long as I brought my lunch from home and didn't have to wait to buy it in the chaotic lunch line. When I needed to, I went to the bathroom in school. I even stood on stage during the spring concert, though I didn't sing. Sometimes I mouthed the words, and I was up there. I went on a TV show with Dr. Adler called *Keeping Kids Healthy*. He was asked to talk about SM on the show, and he had my parents and me come as well. I only said one sentence.

Gym class and recess were still sometimes difficult, but no one bothered me about it. I met with the school psychologist once a week, and a few times a week I went to the resource room. A woman from the resource room came to class with me a few times a week as well, to help me with my work and to make me practice writing. She mostly helped me with my confidence so I would be more comfortable with whatever I was doing. I always felt calmer when she was there.

Chapter 7

Talking Is Hard

In fourth grade, I stopped seeing Dr. Adler every week. Some days were still hard, but my mom and I learned to deal with *it*. I went to see him once in a while during "transition periods," like school breaks and between grades. We called these visits "booster shots." My mom still drove me to school and did everything she could to help me push through *it*. When I didn't want to do something, she would ask me, "What would Dr. Adler say?" I knew what this meant. She came up with the idea based on the rubber bracelets that people were wearing at the time that said, "WWJD?" (meaning "What would Jesus do?"). She was a member of the PTA for almost all of elementary school. She came on all the field trips and school events so I would feel calmer. I eventually asked her not to be involved in school events.

One late spring day in fifth grade, it was extremely hot—I remember how hot it was because I can't take the heat at all. I don't like to sweat. I despise New York summers. The humidity is terrible, and the schools I attended didn't have air conditioning. It was like walking through soup, like I was being cooked from the outside in.

I remember not feeling well that morning. My parents were always skeptical when I said I didn't feel well, but I wasn't faking it. My anxiety actually made me feel sick. Early on, it was hard to tell the difference between the anxiety and physical illness, but I got better at telling them apart. On one visit to Dr. Adler, I asked him, "How do I know if my stomach hurts because I'm sick or if it's because of my anxiety? They feel the same."

He said, "That's a great question," which wasn't an answer because there is no exact answer.

By fifth grade, I got good at telling the two apart, but I was still skeptical of myself. Nowadays, I get the gist of *it*, because I've had to decipher *it* for fifteen years.

What usually happened was that I would tell my parents that I didn't feel well. My mom would try what she could to make me go to school. She would say something like, "Why don't you just get out of bed and try? You might start to feel better," and "If you don't feel good at school, you can go to the nurse. I'll come get you, honey, okay?" That last one usually got me to go. And the "okay?" was never really a question. She knew that if she at least got me through the door, there was a pretty good chance that I would stay the day. The thing was that my teachers and the school nurses knew that I would say I didn't feel well because of *it*. They were all warned by my parents to try everything they could to make me stay in school. I would go to the nurse with stomach pains and nausea, so no one believed me when I was actually sick.

I was never faking sick to stay home. To me, it was real. But that was the problem; it was real. My brain was making my body feel sick.

That day, my mom drove me to school. I remember her telling me again that if I needed her to pick me up, she would. I was okay during the day, but I didn't feel that well. My stomach was bothering me, and my throat hurt a little. They all thought it was just *it* because *it* always made me feel like I wanted to throw up and die. During lunch, I went to the nurse for the first time that day. I read a sign on her door that said that the nurse's office was for *"EMERGENCIES ONLY."* The sign was in all capital letters in red font and was also bolded and italicized. What qualifies as an emergency for an elementary school kid? I second-guessed myself before walking in because I didn't like it when adults yelled at me. I would just cry, and I wouldn't be able to stop myself, which made *it* worse.

I knew the nurse, and she knew me very well. Most of the time, she wasn't very nice. I'm not sure if it was just to me or if she was always like that. She had this look when I came in, a very similar look to the look the teachers and my mom would give me when I didn't want to do something or was being "stubborn." I would never have used that word stubborn, but I know that's what they thought.

She took my temperature and sent me back to lunch. I didn't say anything. I was too scared. She reminded me about the sign on the door. I just stuck it out. It wasn't an emergency. I went back downstairs to class, and we went outside for recess. Normally, we went out the front of the school, but this day we went to the playground in the back. To go outside, we went through two big red metal doors with silver handles that were always cold to the touch. When we went outside in the back, I always stood next to those doors. The teachers never let me stay inside. I just stood there watching everybody, waiting for recess to be over. I don't know why we went outside that day, considering it was extremely hot. I'm surprised no one fainted, but I guess most little kids don't care. I always liked it when it was raining or snowing because we had indoor recess. Two of the classrooms had a mechanical wall that would fold up onto itself, and we would have recess in the same place. I was happy because I got to stay inside. I was probably the only kid who'd rather stay inside, or so it seemed.

Depending on what grade I was in, everyone changed what they did during recess, as if they universally agreed on what would be "cool" that year. This year, basketball was the cool thing, and I watched the other boys play. The girls rarely played with them. Once in a while some of the girls joined in, but it was always the girls who were tomboyish, and it never lasted.

When it was finally time to go back inside, the teacher called, "Recess is over!" One or two kids always followed her in, yelling like Energizer bunnies. I always thought this was funny and laughed silently to myself.

I opened the door and walked inside. I was usually the first one in because it took the teacher time to get the boys to stop doing whatever they were doing. I was hot and sweaty, and I hadn't done anything. Everyone else came in dripping and drank water. By this time, I really didn't feel well. My throat was killing me, and I wanted to throw up. Even though it was hot, I started to shiver. But I didn't do anything because the nurse said to come for emergencies only. This didn't seem like an emergency. I wasn't dying.

One of the kids at my cluster of desks pointed out that I was shivering. The desks were arranged in groups of four or six in a rectangle. I didn't mind that the kid said something. I thought it was pretty funny that I was shivering on one of the hottest days. I knew it probably had something to do with my not feeling well. One of the other kids said I was faking it, and he tried to shiver to show that I was faking. Then the teacher told us we were going to watch a movie—a science clip—and the special education class joined us to watch it.

There were three or four regular classes for the grade and one special education class that these other kids were in. We all thought special education kids were "slow." One of the kids, Neil, sat next to me. We weren't friends. We knew each other because it wasn't a big school, and we were in the same grade. Our brothers happened to be friends and also were in the same grade. All this time, I was feeling really sick and nervous because I didn't know what to do. I didn't want to get yelled at by the nurse. Neil started making fun of me for shivering. I didn't mind because it wasn't in a mean way. If it had been someone else, I probably would've become angry and uncomfortable. Neil was more of an outsider. He wasn't quiet, like I was, but he wasn't like everyone else either. We talked for a little while, but it was mostly him making fun of me.

After a few minutes, the teacher started the movie. I walked over to her desk in the corner of the room and asked her if I could go to the nurse. This teacher was particularly nice to me. When she had taught third grade, my brother was in her class. When she switched to fifth grade a few years later, she became my teacher. She let me go upstairs to the nurse.

I ran down the gray hallway as if I were escaping. Maybe I was speed-walking. And I was shivering. I pulled open the big red doors and ran up the stairs, two at a time. I pulled open the door to the main office and ran to the nurse's office. At the door, I paused and once again read the sign: "The school nurse is for *EMERGENCIES ONLY!*" This time, I turned the knob, slowly opening the door, and saw the nurse's blank face. I started to cry. Her blank face quickly turned into a caring motherly look. She asked me what was wrong. I told her my throat hurt and I couldn't stop shivering. She immediately took my temperature— it was 102.8 degrees. She asked me to lie down, and she turned off the lights. She called my mom and told her to come get me. She placed an ice pack on my head to cool me down. She asked why I hadn't come earlier. I stayed quiet. I wasn't angry, just upset—at her, at myself, at the world.

Toward the end of fifth grade, my parents wanted me to ride the bus to school, which I hadn't been on in the two years since my brother went to middle school. I wanted a fish tank and wanted to raise fish like I did in computer games. I wanted the fish tank to be my reward for getting on the bus. On one of the last days of fifth grade, I thought of getting on the bus as practice for getting on the bus in middle school the following year. At the end of the day, instead of waiting for my mom, grandfather, or grandmother to pick me up, I went to where all the buses were lined up. I remembered from when I was with my brother that ours was the one with the silver flag—a small triangle piece of construction paper wrapped in tin foil. I saw the flag and got on the bus. The bus driver didn't ask who I was, but I saw her look at me when I walked on. She thought I was with the person in front of me. I walked straight to the back and sat in the last seat on the left.

The school wasn't big, and neither was my neighborhood, so I knew or had seen all of the kids before. They said hi to me, which made me feel better. One girl saw me and said to the other kids, "Hey, look! Jon's on the bus." I hated when people pointed things out like that because it drew more attention than I wanted, which was basically none. But before I knew it, the bus was at my bus stop. I saw my mom through the window. I got off, and we went straight to the pet store. I chose a big fish tank, but my pets, other than my first hamsters, usually didn't last very long. I would take care of the pet for a few weeks and then get bored with it, and my dad would have to deal with it.

Chapter 8

Bright Lights

My dad's brother was a police officer in the New York Police Department and later moved to Las Vegas to become a cop there. He wanted a change of pace, and Las Vegas was booming then. The cops in Henderson, a suburb of Las Vegas, were some of the highest paid in the country. He was nine years younger than my dad and seemed more like an older brother to Justin and me than an uncle. He is very much of a go-getter and always is looking for something to do. He opened a tanning salon in New York City with a friend and started a community policing company. In Vegas, he tried working in real estate. He'd always say, "If you don't ask, the answer is always no."

Once he moved to Las Vegas, my grandparents visited him a few times a year. visited him for the first time in the summer I was turning ten. Justin had gone out before me, and he seemed to have a good time, going to arcades, seeing all the hotels, and swimming in the pools. My grandparents went for three weeks each summer. My parents knew that three weeks was too long a time for me to go, and I didn't want to stay that long anyway. So the plan was that I would fly out with my grandparents, and in a few days, my dad would come out and then fly back with me.

My trip to Vegas was the first time I was away from my parents for an extended period. I had spent nights at my grandparents' house in Queens but not for very long. The first time I tried staying over with my grandparents, my dad had to drive an hour to come pick me up in the middle of the night.

Another time, we went to visit my great-grandmother, and for some reason, I did not want to go at all. They forced me to go, and I panicked in the car on the way there. Inside her house, to the left of the front door, were the steps to go upstairs. I just lay there in a ball and cried. I eventually cried myself to exhaustion and fell asleep. When I woke up, I wouldn't talk to anyone for a while.

There wasn't much evidence to show that I would be able to handle being three thousand miles away, but for some reason I wanted to go, and they let me. I was a little older than I was when I didn't do well those times in Queens.

My visit went well for a few days, but one night I broke down—something triggered it—locked myself in the bedroom, and cried. I called my dad on the phone nonstop. When he hung up, I would just call back. I wanted him to come get me. He told me he'd be there in a few days, that he couldn't come now. I didn't think I could wait that long.

Also, the temperature in Las Vegas in the summer can rise to 120 degrees by the middle of the day. I couldn't stay outside for more than a few minutes at a time. Every place had really good air conditioning, so when I wasn't sweating to death, I felt like I was in Alaska.

After that time, I promised myself I would never go to Las Vegas again. But as the years passed, my grandparents and uncle tried to get me to go back. I eventually realized that I wanted to prove to myself that I could do it.

This time I appreciated Vegas because I was ready. I was more comfortable in my own skin. And after the second try, I began going every summer for three weeks at a time, and some years I even went out for another week during school breaks.

I was more capable of allowing myself to have the experience. We ate out a lot and went to arcades, cool museums, shows, and hotels. For one of the first times, I felt free and that I could do anything I wanted. No one was looking at me. I wouldn't see anyone I knew. I didn't need to be on DEFCON 1. It was great, and I felt good being someplace other than home.

One night when we were driving back to my uncle's house from downtown, I was staring out the car window at all the lights and the hotels. One of the hotels, the Luxor, is shaped like a pyramid with a light on top that supposedly can be seen from space. Another hotel is shaped like a section of the New York City skyline, and there's one that is a replica of the Eiffel Tower. The hotels are tall, brightly colored, and lit up twenty-four/seven. I was in awe. I muttered, "I don't know why anyone would want to leave this place."

When I was thirteen, during one of the summers I was in Vegas, my uncle surprised me for my birthday with an introductory flight lesson. I had always been interested in planes but never thought about actually flying them. We went to an airport in the middle of the desert. It must have been 115 degrees with the sun shining. We met the pilot who was going to take us up. He was big, and the planes were small. When I first saw the plane, it was kind of puzzling to me how it could fly.

I got in and sat in the pilot's seat. I could barely see over the hood of the plane. My uncle sat in the back, and the instructor sat in the copilot's seat up front. We wore those big, bulky headsets so we could hear each other without all the engine noise. I watched the pilot get everything started. It was a short flight, but he tried to explain some of the stuff that he was doing. We taxied out to the runway as he spoke to someone through the headset. It seemed almost like another language. We hurdled down the runway, and the pilot told me to put my hands on the controls. He told me when to pull up. He had his hands on his controls and guided me along. He said, "Congratulations. You just took off your first plane."

I was excited and in awe of the experience. We were in the air, flying over the peach-gray sand, suspended over the ground. All I could do was look outside. It seemed as if we were all alone and in complete control. It was pure bliss. The world seemed smaller and gigantic at the same time—almost as if our significance in the world changed in some unknown, insignificant way.

When I got back home to New York, flying was all I could think about. I convinced my dad to let me take flying lessons. I was seventeen, the youngest age allowed by law, when I earned my pilot's license.

Part 2
Middle School

Chapter 9

The Bridge

Transitioning to middle school was rough. I was finally beginning to feel at least okay at school, and then it was all taken away, and something new was shoved in my face. The older kids in the middle school were notorious for being assholes to the younger kids, so the school placed all sixth-graders in A-wing. D-wing and C-wing were for seventh- and eighth-graders, depending on where in the district they lived. B-wing was the cafeteria, gym, and elective classrooms. E-wing was another gym and more elective classrooms. Twelve elementary schools in the district fed into this one middle school. Depending on the year, more than two thousand kids could be in the school. For someone who's afraid of people, it was basically a nightmare. I know it was a nightmare for a lot of other people too.

We anticipated I would have a problem with it. I hadn't seen Dr. Adler in a while so we made an appointment to see him before the start of school to prepare. I didn't want to go see him. We had to drive to the city to see him at ESU. By this time, he embodied memories and feelings of the past. He was "contaminated." I didn't want to think about them now, nor did I want to think about going to middle school. I protested, but my mom insisted that we go. I sat in the front passenger seat, crying and screaming. My seat belt was suffocating and causing me sheer panic. I unclicked it and threw it off me.

Nothing my mom could have said would have made me feel better. I was breathing very heavily. She tried to calm me down, but nothing worked. We were on a bridge crossing the Hudson River. It was a pretty summer day, which didn't fit my mood. I grabbed the door handle with my left hand, unlocking it at the same time, and pushed the door open with my right hand. I looked down and the white line on the road rushed past as if time were going at the same pace. I didn't have the door open more than six inches before my mom yelled, "Jon!" I'd never heard that tone in her voice. Never have I since. It was fear, yelling, and crying, all in one.

I quickly shut the door. My heart shot into my throat. I rushed to put on my seat belt to put pressure on me. I didn't say or do anything for the rest of the ride. My mom continued to drive and cry. She told me never to do that again. I had threatened before to jump out of the car on the way to elementary school, but I had never opened the door. This time, we were on a busy bridge, going eighty miles an hour, at least two hundred feet above the Hudson River.

Once at Dr. Adler's office, we talked about what happened and how hard it was for me to get to his office. All we did was talk, and I was fine. We made a simple plan for getting me to middle school. We made some compromises, and I felt a little better. He gave me a doctor's note so I wouldn't have to do gym as soon as the year started. We planned for my mom and me to talk to the school. She spoke to the guidance counselor, psychologist, and a bunch of other teachers. A couple of days before school started, I went in with my mom and my brother, who had just graduated from eighth grade, to tour the building. The building was huge. I knew I was going to get lost, but they tried to calm me down and show me the tricks as much as they could. A few of the hallways that went around the buildings would have fewer kids in them, so they showed me those.

On the first day of school, my mom drove me. The bus would've been too much to handle. I made sure my bag was organized, with one binder for each subject. I color-coordinated them. Red for math, green for science, white for English, black for history, and a thinner red one for Spanish. Everything was in its place and had its own spot. My dad laminated my schedule so I could look at it whenever I needed to. He made it the size of a business card, and it fit perfectly in my right pocket.

My first day went pretty well, considering my anticipation that it might not. That happened often. I only got lost once—I couldn't find the library. I walked past it a few times, but there were so many kids standing in front of it that I couldn't tell it was the library. I somehow pulled together the courage to ask someone for help. I made sure to ask a girl because I thought the guys might pick on me. They had a reputation. The girl I asked happened to be very nice and brought me to the library. Funny thing is that she ended up being my mom's coworker's daughter. And I had no idea until weeks later.

The school psychologist, Ms. Valente, was meeting me in the library. My dad had e-mailed with her before school started, and they came up with that plan. She was a very nice woman. She was tall, thin, and had jet black hair. I didn't speak much to her, but I answered her questions when she asked. We made a time for me to see her once a week during lunch, with one or two other kids. I always looked forward to going because it was time away from the crowd. We usually just talked and played board games. It was a good distraction. She told me that whenever I needed to, I could come see her. She still remembers that I always wore comfy sweatshirts, even when it was hot outside.

Once a week, I also went to the middle school's version of the resource room with the other kids. There were two teachers there that helped us with whatever we needed. One of the two teaching assistants was also always in all of my academic classes. It never felt like she was there for us; it was more like she was an extra teacher in class. They both were always very nice. For tests, I went to another room with one of them. I never used the extra time they gave me, but I felt much better being away.

Sixth and seventh grades went off without any real problems. Once we got the system in place, it was okay. Gym was always a pain in the ass, but I had the doctor's notes to get me out of gym.

I still didn't have many friends, and I was always ready to leave when the day ended. I always wanted it to end. I didn't like times like lunch, when I had to be with other kids. I would just sit with some kids I knew from elementary school or sometimes by myself to do work. I always preferred to do my work by myself. Group work seemed unnecessary and slowed me down.

As I got older, I had to do presentations in class. In elementary school, the teachers all knew to leave me alone. But the time had come when the teachers couldn't let me do whatever I wanted anymore. I was deathly afraid of my first presentation. I spent the start of the day with Ms. Valente, who spoke to the teachers. She made a deal with the science teacher to let me stand there this time and not say anything. The teacher agreed, but I didn't even want to do that. I didn't want to stand up in front of everyone. It was just pointless to me. Somehow they convinced me to stand there. They might have threatened to give me a zero for my grade. Getting good grades was the one thing I was good at. It was sometimes enough of a push. Ms. Valente also closed her door on me.

In seventh grade, most of my classes were in D-wing. I had all new teachers. The only good thing was that Ms. Valente's office was in the same wing. On my first day of seventh grade, I was walking from homeroom to my first class next to another kid, Dylan, who I knew from the year before in the resource room. We were talking when one of his friends came up to him on the right and started talking to him. They seemed like good friends. I noticed the kid had a stutter. I didn't say anything. I heard the kid say to Dylan, "Don't talk to him. He's fat." I don't think he meant for me to hear it, but I did. Dylan had a sad, awkward look on his face and walked away with him.

I ended up being in a few classes with both of them. I didn't know what to think or how to feel. Both of them were in special classes, just like me. I didn't expect it from them, especially because one of them had a stutter and was probably picked on. He should've known how it felt.

I became a lot more self-conscious that year about the way I looked and about my grades and friends. One day I came home from school, went into the back room, and cried on the couch. My mom came in, and I cried to her that I had no friends. She started to cry too. She named some of the kids I knew, and I said something like, "They aren't my friends. I don't talk to anyone in school." We cried for an hour. I eventually got over it, and the weeks went by, just like they always did.

My mom and dad had to drive me to school a lot because I refused to go on the bus or purposely missed the bus. Often I felt so uncomfortable that I would have to change sixteen times and then would stare at myself in the mirror. That wasn't on purpose, but it made me miss the bus a lot. Other times I just couldn't get myself to move.

Around that time, my parents went to an Elton John concert. My dad bought one of the overpriced CDs they were selling for his car. I would listen to it with him on the way to school a lot. We would listen to one song on repeat in the mornings. It was called "The Bridge." In my family it came to be known as my song. It helped to put a lot of things in perspective.

Another day when I got home from school I was just so frustrated with myself. My mom was cooking, and I started crying and breathing heavily, like everything was falling inward into a black hole. I went outside on the deck and spun in circles, watching the world spin by. I grabbed the red wire dog chain that was outside on the table, wrapped it twice around my neck, and pulled it from both ends. I felt the pressure build up in my head. I stopped pulling a little and walked back inside. I stood there in front of my mom.

She was surprisingly calm. She told me to stop, but I pulled harder. She picked up the phone and dialed the number for Child Protective Services. She didn't press the call button, but she dialed the number on the phone. "I will call them if you don't stop," she said, "and they will take you away because I can't handle you anymore."

I yelled, *"Stop!"*

The standoff lasted only for a minute, but it felt like an hour. I eventually let go of the chain and collapsed on the floor, crying. She took the leash and put it in her room. She came back and continued cooking as if nothing had happened. I stayed there on the floor for a while.

The next day, she told me we were going to see Dr. Adler. I wasn't mad this time. In fact, I was happy because it meant I didn't have to go to school. The car ride went well. We listened to music and didn't talk. She never brought up what had happened. When we got to the office, the first question Dr. Adler asked me was, "Do you remember trying to hurt yourself yesterday?"

I got really sad and said, "Yes."

We spoke about it a little. My mom and I went back a few times to meet with him until I felt better. I needed another booster shot.

Chapter 10
To Stand the Test of Time

I vividly remember one day of middle school. It was the first week of eighth grade. At lunchtime, I went into the cafeteria, but I always brought my lunch to school because I was too nervous to buy lunch. My mom always said we pick and choose our battles. As long as I was eating in school, the battle of buying lunch wasn't necessary. The middle school was so big it needed three separate cafeterias. There were three big white and blue square rooms in a line separated by tall glass walls. Two long hallways framed the sides to get from one room to the other and each cafeteria held twenty to thirty rectangular tables. This wasn't enough space. Each grade—sixth, seventh, and eighth—ate during different periods.

I walked into the cafeteria, and the popular kids were sitting to the left of the door along the wall. Sitting at the next table were kids I used to be friends with in elementary school and in sixth grade, when we had some of the same classes. Since then, we hadn't talked much, but I didn't want to sit alone. Sitting alone sometimes made more of a scene than anything else. Sitting with them was the not-so-bad option. The first day wasn't so bad. I didn't really talk to them. I just listened and ate my turkey sandwich on potato bread.

The following day I was less nervous because I knew I had somewhere to sit. I arrived a little early and sat at the same table. The room slowly filled up, and some of the same kids came back to the table. I stayed seated at the end of the table, close to the glass wall, so I could see people walking in the hallways and in the door.

After a few minutes, more kids showed up. For some reason, everyone who was at the table just left and went to sit in one of the other cafeterias. We were supposed to stay in the cafeteria we were assigned, but no one listened to that rule. The one kid I knew from elementary school said to me, "Sorry, Jon," and left. I didn't know what to do, so I stayed by myself and ate my lunch. It was pretty funny, an ironic sense. I went out of my way—for one of the first times—not to be the kid who was always by himself. It worked for one day but not the next. Everyone left, and I was back to where I started.

I stayed at the table by myself for a few weeks. I started to do homework during lunch so I wasn't staring into space by myself. After a while, I got sick of it. One day some of the popular kids at the table in front of me were talking. I knew some of them from elementary school too. We had been friends when we were little, but we'd grown distant as time went on. They were asking about who was sitting at the empty table next to them. A kid said, "That's not an empty table. Jon sits there."

The next day I went back to that table and ate my lunch. Every day when I went to throw out my garbage, I passed by Neil from elementary school. That day I wanted to ask him if I could sit with him, but he wasn't there. I asked the other kids if I could sit there, and I just sat down. One of the kids pointed to the other end of the table and said, "Neil sits on that side." I moved to the other end of the table.

I just didn't know what I had done to make so many kids not want to even acknowledge me when they saw me. I never bothered anyone. I had to be one of the least annoying kids in school. I never talked to anyone. I never did anything. I think people were "scared" of quiet people. Maybe people think something is wrong with loners, like they're crazy or messed up. Or that quiet people are someplace else. Maybe they just didn't like me because I was different. For the rest of eighth grade, however, I sat with Neil and the other kids.

That may have been the first time that I stopped and thought about life, myself, who I was, and what it meant, if it meant anything at all. This might have been the moment I realized that something was off—not with me but with life.

That may seem very cynical, but I think there are multiple points in our lives when we question what we think about ourselves and what we think about the people around us. This was the first time I did that.

Chapter 11

The New Guy

Throughout eighth grade *it* started to get progressively worse. Sometimes, for what seems like no reason at all, that happens. *It* seems to naturally come and go in cycles. I couldn't stand my middle school. In January, I kind of gave up. I couldn't get out of the house much. I was afraid I would see kids I knew from school. I refused to go out to dinner with my parents and brother. I only left the house for school. My mom knew that I needed to go to the doctor again.

When I was little, whenever my parents went out without me, I would stay home with my grandparents. As my parents were leaving, I would scream and cry, running all over the house, trying to block the exits. I would stand by the staircase leading to the front door, with my arms spread out between the wall and the railing, blocking their path, but they would just go out another door if they couldn't get me to move. Once they left, I would collapse on the floor, sometimes not even crying. But that's what had to happen.

By this time, I didn't care about anything. I was more robotic than I usually was and more so at home than ever.

It was kind of strange seeing my doctor again after two or three years. After only one session, Dr. Adler recommended somebody else for me to see because I felt uncomfortable with him. I also felt uncomfortable about seeing someone new and about telling him my story, instead of working with someone who already knew what I went through. I wasn't ready to replay all those memories with a stranger.

My father and I went to see a new doctor, which was strange because I always dealt with this stuff with my mother. It was kind of like because I had a new doctor, a new parent was dealing with me. That was nerve-wracking all by itself. I never really spoke about *it* with my dad. I guess he wasn't comfortable talking about *it* with me either. My dad and I didn't say much in the car on the way to the doctor. I remember the building, the elevator ride with my dad, the cramped office, and the doctor. The building was a regular office building. I would not have known it was a doctor's office.

There was one other kid in the waiting room. I didn't know why he was there, and he didn't know why I was there. Neither of us cared. Around the room were a bunch of pamphlets about different disorders. "Does your kid have problems going to school?" "Does your child have problems focusing?" "Does your child have problems socializing?" I knew I had a problem, just like other kids knew they had problems. For some reason, all those pamphlets made me angry and upset. It just seemed like it was done in the wrong way, like they were trying to fit these kids into a mold.

I heard the doctor call my name, and we went into a small room with a desk, three chairs, and plenty more pamphlets. My father and the doctor about spent twenty minutes talking about me and my problems in the past and my problems at that time. Afterward, the doctor asked me questions about why I refused to go to school. I didn't have much to say to the guy. He just seemed so fake and not genuine. I wanted to get the hell out of there.

We didn't get much accomplished in our session, but the doctor re-prescribed my old medication. It had helped in the past, so I was ready to try it again. I also knew that I didn't want to start over again with someone new. During the car ride home, I told my father that I did not want to see the new doctor and was fine going back to Dr. Adler.

The following week, I began seeing Dr. Adler again at ESU. He was willing to work with me again as long as I was willing to start working. After my first session, he spoke to my mom and me about my writing a daily journal about when I got "the feeling" and got anxious. I had to write down what I was doing and the time of day and rate my anxiety on a scale of one to seven. I was not excited by the idea.

Chapter 12

The Next Day One

When the next week came, my mom picked me up early from school to see Dr. Adler. I remembered about the journal on the way there. I hadn't really been working on the journal and had left it at home. I began rewriting on paper my mom had in the car what I had written over the past week. I had nothing to say. The moments I should have written about were not clear, and I didn't see the point of writing whatever I remembered of my level of anxiety from a week ago.

I didn't have much to show Dr. Adler. I was nervous about what he would say, and what he did say made me realize the only way I'd get better was to really work at it. Nowadays, I say that you can't help people who don't want to help themselves. And that was true for me at that moment. Dr. Adler had little reason to help me if I wasn't putting in the effort to help myself. The problem was I didn't really want to put in the effort. I just wanted *it* to go away forever.

I saw Dr. Adler in an office close to my house; sometimes, he came to my house, as long as I'd made the effort. We talked about many things, including the topic of talking on the telephone. I hated speaking to people, especially strangers, on the phone. I never answered the phone if I did not recognize the phone number on the caller ID. I also never called anyone except my parents.

In one session, Dr. Adler asked me to call my local library to see what time it closed.

"I can just look it up on the Internet," I told him. "Who cares what time they close? I have no interest in going to the library."

We argued for twenty minutes over why I should call, and I kept insisting it was unnecessary.

Through all the arguing, however, he helped me realize how *it* was getting in the way. I began working more seriously on my journal, sometimes multiple times a day. To this day I can't look at a black-and-white composition notebook without thinking about my anxiety journal. I can't stand those notebooks anymore.

For the next couple of months, I kept my journal and met with Dr. Adler weekly. I found myself slowly getting better, but I still had lots of problems in school.

Chapter 13

A Little Too Much

I never really participated in gym. When I was very little, I had a note from my psychologist, stating that I could not participate because it could be "detrimental" to my progress. Later, in elementary and middle school, I had a doctor's note for physical reasons—I had a problem with my heels. If I did too much physical exercise I would get sharp pains in my legs. Later on, this became an excuse to get out of gym because I wasn't ready for it. To this day, I get extreme panic attacks when doing something that I am not used to doing. It's the same with my having to "perform" with or in front of others.

In January of eighth grade, my doctor's note expired. By coincidence, we'd just ended our unit in the school pool. When the teacher found out my note had expired, he thought the note was only to get out of swimming, like it was a scam or something. He was always yelling at students. The school psychologists spoke to him a few times about yelling in general but got nowhere. I spoke to my parents and Ms. Valente, telling them I couldn't participate in gym class. My dad spoke to the doctor who originally had given me the doctor's note and told him that I was having problems in school. My dad asked if he would re-prescribe the note. The doctor wrote me the note.

I was too afraid to hand the gym teacher the note. I didn't want to go to school that day, so we were late. My parents had notified Ms. Valente, and she met us in the parking lot. I spent almost the entire day in or waiting outside Ms. Valente's office as she tried to calm me down. I went to a couple of classes but kept going back to her office. In her office, I kept calling my parents, trying to convince them to pick me up. Ms. Valente let me do it because she knew they would say no.

Later in the day, she had meetings in other parts of the school. Before leaving her office, she told me, "You can't stay in my office, but you can wait outside until gym. When it's time for gym, you have to give the teacher the note."

On the way to gym class, I noticed the note was filled out but under "name," it was blank. The gym teacher asked me questions in his loud voice. I needed to disappear. Everyone was staring at us as he was trying to intimidate me. I felt like he thought I was faking it or that the note was fake. He told me that the note wasn't good. He told that I had to participate and seemed really frustrated. I left the gym and I walked as fast as I could to Ms. Valente's office. I told her what had happened.

"I'm surprised," she said. "I've spoken to him numerous times about you."

"Are you sure you talked to the right person? He acted the same way he always does."

That was the last time I went to gym class in middle school.

I was in a health class in another wing of the school. Most of my classes were in D-wing, which had about six hundred students. For health class, though, I was placed in C-wing with six hundred students I had never seen before. It was like transferring to an entirely new school with six hundred new kids. Now, instead of just being with all the new people, I also had to interact with them. I was able to tolerate my other classes without actively participating, but in health class we had group activities. I had to participate.

I refused to go to school on days when I had health class or gym, or I would go to Ms. Valente's office until the period was over so I didn't have to deal with those classes. It wasn't a good thing to do but I was drowning. Science class was an issue on lab days. I was in advanced science and math classes. Both were in the other wing, as was my Spanish class. We weren't assigned lab partners for science; we had to choose our partners, but I knew no one in the class. A lot of the other kids knew each other already. I was always left not knowing who to be with, and the kids weren't always the nicest. More than half my classes were with kids I had never spoken to and, in most cases, had never seen. That year, I missed most of the first part of the second semester because *it* was so bad, and I didn't want to go to school.

I spoke to the principal about my health and Spanish classes, but he said health class was required by law. He offered to switch me to D-wing for Spanish so I would know some of the kids. I asked which students were in the Spanish class. He said he was not allowed to tell me, but Ms. Valente might tell me who was on the class roster. I didn't understand why he couldn't tell me because if I walked by the class while it was happening, I would be able to see who was in the class.

Later that week I met with Ms. Valente. She told me who was in the class and mentioned a kid named Bryan. I knew immediately that I didn't want to be in that class. He was one of the kids who'd teased me in other classes and during lunch in the previous year.

"I don't want to be in the class," I said.

"I'll make sure that you sit far away from Bryan and that the teacher knows not to put you together," she responded.

I still refused. The funny thing was that he was new the year before. I had seen him sitting alone during lunch and had gone over to sit with him with another kid. He was also on my bus. We sat together for the rest of the year. But by eighth grade, he never left me alone and always picked on me.

I never went to the new Spanish class and nothing ever happened with health class. I kept seeing Dr. Adler and Ms. Valente. Many days, I refused to go to school. I stopped going with my parents to the mall or out to dinner, scared that I would see someone from school. My parents never stopped trying to get me to go to school, but I couldn't get over things that were happening. I just felt like I was so alone but I also wanted to be left alone by everyone because everything made me nervous. My mother would drive me to school because I refused to take the bus. My mom chose her battles carefully, and forcing me to take the bus was not one of them. Some days my mom couldn't deal with it, or she couldn't do it by herself. I always knew that when the front door opened again in the mornings, it was my dad coming back from work to try to get me to go to school.

I told my parents I did not want to go to school. My dad offered to start paying me again to go to school—twenty dollars for every day I went. But this time, I just couldn't do it. Every little thing annoyed me. Things were piling up, and so much was getting to me. It's amazing how the littlest things can have such a big impact, and nobody else can see them except the person feeling them.

Part 3
A Better Place

Chapter 14

The First Day of the Rest of My Life

Dr. Adler had the idea that I should transfer schools. His wife worked at a private school that was ten minutes from my house. He suggested that my parents look into it as an option for me. In some ways, I saw it as giving up on the fight, like I was taking the easy way out. But I also saw it as maybe a new beginning.

That night, after seeing Dr. Adler, I spoke about the Magnolia Day School with my parents. We researched the school on the Internet, and my dad received information by fax from the head of admissions. I liked what I read about the school, especially the small class sizes. The school had about 130 students, pre-K through twelfth grade, with about twenty teachers. Instead of six hundred kids in my grade, there'd be fewer than twenty. Later, I found out that it was only eight.

The school was on twenty-acre campus that used to be a farm. I was nervous because I needed performing arts credits to graduate. My parents, on the other hand, were nervous about paying an extra thirty thousand dollars for me to go to school, but they were willing to pay if it meant I would physically go to school and feel better doing it.

The next time I met with Dr. Adler, we spoke again about Magnolia Day School. I told him that I thought it was a good idea. I never told him that I felt like I was giving up on the fight by leaving the other school. I never told anyone about that. "I'm surprised you suggested it," I told him.

"It's different than you telling me that you want to be homeschooled," he said. "Being homeschooled would be giving up. You would get worse if you never were forced to leave the house."

I went to visit MDS on a weekend with my mom and Dr. Adler. He knew the head of the school and head of admissions, so they allowed him to show me around. There were five buildings on the campus: the middle school, high school, library, art building, and children's school and cafeteria. First, we went into the high school. The classrooms were small, and I liked that a driver's ed class was going on in one of the classrooms. We walked past the head of admissions' office. I saw my application folder on his desk, along with a few others. I tried to look at it, but my mom and Dr. Adler stopped me. We walked around the rest of the campus and then left. Dr. Adler wanted me to visit again during the school day. I agreed, and my dad set up an appointment for me to follow another student around from class to class.

A few days later, I was in eighth-grade homeroom at MDS. I was excited but very nervous. *It* started to take control, and I asked my dad if I could just visit for a half day instead. I wanted to be picked up before lunch. I kept bugging him, so he called Dr. Adler. Dr. Adler quickly said no, that I had to stay for the entire day. My anxieties lessened somewhat, and I actually did enjoy some of the day. The best part: I missed a day at my real school.

For my visit, I was paired with an eighth-grader, Lucia. Her mom was the Spanish teacher at the school. Lucia was on the shorter side and had dark brown hair. She was kind of pale, and whenever she spoke Spanish to her mom, her accent seemed to have a lisp. I met a bunch of kids that day, some from my grade and some who were older and younger. They were all very nice to me and asked me questions about where I was from and other things. At the end of the day, the teacher had the kids help to move chairs from the cafeteria to the band room because of an upcoming performance. So, on my first day, the school had me doing physical labor. That could have been a sign in itself, but it wasn't. I really liked all the teachers and that was very important because I wanted more than what my other school was giving me. They all seemed genuine, unlike a lot of other teachers and students that I had met before.

Once the day ended, I knew that I wanted to go back. At MDS, no one knew I was "the kid who doesn't speak." They only knew me as the new kid. I could have been anyone I wanted to be. The fact that I was the weird, shy kid didn't matter. I transferred into the school a few days later, thanks to my dad.

Chapter 15

A New Beginning

New starts don't come around very often, but it's important that we notice them when they happen. The first few weeks at my new school were pretty good. Just the fact that it was a new place probably helped the most, but having only five to ten kids in each of my classes made it even easier. If I had to do it all over again, I would have convinced my parents to send me there sooner. I quickly made "friends." I guess it's easy to find friends when there aren't many options. There were only two boys in my class: one Korean American, Jake; and one from South Korea, Dong-Jin. I wasn't sure I liked the Dong-Jin, maybe because he was quiet himself; maybe he was afraid that he would mess up when speaking English. Jake was also on the quiet side at times, but he seemed to be very immature, almost as if he were stuck in the mind of a younger kid, especially in the things he did and said and in the questions he asked other people.

Some people might find silence comforting, but to me, as a quiet person, other quiet people scare me. I "interact" more easily with louder, "crazy" people because they always talk to me. And I respond. I don't have to initiate talk with them. With quieter people, both of us are scared to talk. The conversation goes nowhere.

Because the two other boys in my grade also were quiet, I hung out with the two girls in my grade, Lucia and Anya. Both looked out for me because I was new. Lucia and Anya were good friends. Anya was one of the very few black kids in the school. She was always nice to me. She was very smart and always had chapped lips. There were a few other girls in my class, but I didn't really talk to them, and they didn't talk to me. I always sat with

Anya and/or Jake during lunch on the wooden bleachers on the side of the gym. Most of the other kids sat in the middle at folding tables.

We didn't talk much during lunch. We usually ate and then did schoolwork. Jake was always trying to talk to me about video games, especially war games. There was another international student in my grade from Korea. Her name was Ji-Woo, and she didn't talk to me much either. She and Dong-Jin were supposedly dating.

Coming from a place where I'd felt alone in the crowd of two thousand kids, one or two friends was enough. And really I didn't care about having friends. All I cared about was going to school every day and feeling okay doing that.

I also liked my classes, except maybe English class with Ms. Evans. I felt bad for her. She didn't know how to control our class. Sometimes the kids picked on her. She also had a lazy eye, which didn't help at all.

The only "mean" kids were the seventh-grade boys. They weren't so much mean as just annoying and rambunctious. Lucia and Anya told me on my first day to stay away from them. "If you stay away, they'll leave you alone," Lucia said. On my first day, the five boys tried to talk to me; they asked for my Xbox Live account. I gave it to them. I didn't see any harm. They were all smart, and I was impressed by them, especially in English and history. Mostly, I stayed away from them, as much as that was possible in a middle school of fewer than forty kids. Only years later did I get to know some of them.

One of the girls in the seventh grade, Ava, talked to me a lot during recess. She was nice but very energetic and sometimes annoying. She was very pretty, tall, and had long black hair. She got on my nerves sometimes from talking too much. One day, she drank from a bottle of Hershey's chocolate syrup. But anyone who talked to me and wasn't mean was someone who I usually liked.

History with Mr. Anthony became my favorite class. He was an actor who apparently had decided acting wasn't for him. His acting experience helped him a lot with his teaching. Relatively boring topics in European Renaissance history were more interesting in his class. He seemed like he really cared and was interested in the topics he was teaching. A lot of the classes were split up into A and B classes—B supposedly was more advanced than A. A lot of the grades were so small that they usually combined grades for classes—like 7/8 B history, which I had with Anya and the seventh-grade boys.

Eventually, the being-new feeling wore off, and I kind of lost my motivation to go to school again. It wasn't the same feeling as before—of not wanting to go to school or being too nervous to go. This time, it was more a being bored kind of feeling. I think it was all part of a cycle. I still didn't do things outside of school. No clubs, friends, or whatever. At the time, I was okay with that because I didn't know any better.

At the end of the year, the school held a graduation ceremony. It was a moving-up ceremony that was unnecessary and tacky. I could have seen some meaning in it if we were leaving the place forever, but we weren't. It was just like any other year. I think it was a ploy to get the families to feel proud of their kids and for them to feel good about the school. I really didn't want to go.

Everyone knew I didn't want to go, and the kids, my teachers, and my parents told me I had to go. Of course I didn't actually have to go because that was my decision. But I knew that it would mean a lot to my parents, and it would look strange if I wasn't there. I had to go, and I definitely knew it.

All eight of us in the eighth grade got to decide which song would play as we walked to the stage during the ceremony. We had to come to a collective decision with our homeroom teacher, Ms. Morgan. We searched online and on YouTube on the Smart Board during many homeroom days. One song we came across was "How Far We've Come" by Matchbox Twenty. As soon as I heard it, I knew this should be the song. It seemed very fitting for me, and I knew it had to be meaningful to the other kids because everyone has a story. Everyone goes through things, and shit happens whether we like it or not. I kept badgering the teacher that this had to be the song, and the class agreed because it was one of those songs that everyone liked.

It was also a tradition that during the ceremony, each of the students had to do something, like play an instrument, read a poem, or give a speech. Ms. Morgan kept saying that this was our time, though I didn't really know what we'd done to deserve it. Some kids made a photo slideshow; others wrote a poem with each of our names and words to describe us for each letter. The two Korean students read a poem in Korean.

This wasn't something I had to do, so I chose not to do anything—until our last meeting before graduation. One of the other girls, Andrea, kept telling Ms. Morgan that it would be a good idea for me to read the poem in English that Ji-Woo and Dong-Jin were going to read in Korean. Ms. Morgan either didn't hear her or was ignoring her because she knew I didn't want to do it. Andrea continued to repeat her idea, and every time she did, I grew more frustrated. I wanted this bitch to worry about herself and just leave me alone.

But we can't worry about ourselves all the time. Sometimes, other people need help or need a push, no matter how angry they may be about it or how hard they push back. I told Ms. Morgan that I'd think about it.

During my appointment with Dr. Adler, which was downstairs in my house, where we sat on a giant U-shaped couch, I told him about what happened. I knew what he was going to say because he never told me *not* to do something. He said, knowing my answer, "What do you want to be when you grow up?"

I said, "Business. Maybe be a financial advisor like my dad."

"You won't be able to do that" was his rebuttal.

I thought, *What the fuck are you talking about, and who are you to tell me that?* I actually said, "Why?"

He said, "If you can't talk to people or always want to get out of public speaking, you won't be able to talk to coworkers or clients."

"Yeah," I said. This went on for a few minutes, as my thinking was dragging us in circles. I knew he was right, but I refused to agree. We decided that if I did read the poem, I wouldn't have to see him once a week anymore. I definitely was up for that deal, so I eventually told Ms. Morgan that I would do it. And I did read the poem at graduation. As horrified as I was going into it, I felt pretty good after it was over. But *it*'s never over.

I continued to coast for ninth grade while I finished finding my place and my people. It clearly takes a long time for me to get comfortable somewhere. Only in tenth grade did I join my first club, Varsity Sports Video Production. The funny thing was we didn't have many sports. We only had soccer in the fall and basketball in the winter. But we had this video production team. Instead of videotaping sports games, we videotaped school events, talent shows, and theater productions. There were only two of us who consistently came to the meetings, so we decided to meet during the school day. The teacher, Kevin, was one of the directors of the school play and musical. The two directors were husband and wife. Kevin's wife, Judy, was the main director and handled all the costumes and acting. Kevin helped out with that too, but he was mostly in charge of the set, props, and tech stuff. Their son had gone to the school a while before, but they always came back to do shows at the school.

I enjoyed videotaping and learning how to edit video. The biggest thing was that it forced me to go to after-school events. Previously, I had never gone to school events. The other kid in the club, Jackie, helped me get to know more people at school. She was very friendly with a lot of people at school and very funny.

It was like a domino effect—the more I did after school, the more kids I got to know, the more I liked seeing them, and the more I liked going to school.

Chapter 16

Better?

Before I went off to college, I knew that I needed practice living away from home. As a little kid, I refused to go to sleep-away camp or even to sleepovers at other kids' houses. I knew after ninth grade that I would have to do something. Plus, it would look good on my college application if I took a class over the summer at a college.

I had problems socializing, so I don't know why I thought I wouldn't have the same problems when I was away. Like all the other times, I should have had anticipatory anxiety, but somehow I didn't this time. Expecting that there will be a problem allows me to prepare and not be shocked. But it definitely shocked me and probably put me back a bit in my progress. I was embarrassed that I didn't think I'd have problems, and *it* got pretty bad. And then I felt like a failure.

Before I went to the summer program at Nicholas University, I asked Dr. Adler to write me a letter so I could get a private room and a private bathroom. It took some work, but my parents' persistence and support got it done. That was the one thing I knew I would need.

The drive to Rhode Island was about three and a half hours and very painful for me. I felt like my insides were tearing open. I couldn't concentrate on anything. When I get like that, I also get very stubborn and start to shut down. Everything that happens annoys me. My mom knows my look when it is happening. She also knows she can't do anything to help. It's a lose/lose for us when she says something because no matter what she says, I yell at her.

Checking in was the worst. It's very hard for me to talk to kids my own age because I feel they are more likely to judge me. They are more real to me than someone who is, say, forty years old. Not that forty-year-olds aren't real people, but my brain doesn't see them as much of a threat, as it does with someone my age. Maybe it's because when I do have problems, it's usually with someone my age. Waiting in line to register, I saw someone I knew. My family had gone on a cruise to Alaska the year before, and we met this family. Now, the mother was dropping off her daughter at the summer program. In theory, it would've been nice to be friends with her because then it might not have been as overwhelming. Problem was, I never saw her again after check-in.

After getting my keys and school ID we had to walk over to the dorm I was living in. We didn't know where we were going so they had people helping the kids moving in. That first week I was there was also one of the hottest weeks on record in the Northeast. As I've mentioned, I hate the heat with a passion. I mispronounced the name of my dorm to the kid delivering the mini-refrigerator and microwave I'd rented. He just corrected me and we continued but it made me feel sick for some reason. I remember the pain from my embarrassment. Adrenaline does that to you. When I get the rush of anxiety from situations it almost an identical feeling to when I see a spider. It's an adrenaline rush telling me to get away. My brain just seems to think that I need to run away from people so I don't get hurt.

I once watched a documentary on the Science Channel about mice. When the mice were put into a little pool with a landing in the middle that they could walk on, they just swam in a circle around the perimeter, looking for a way to get out. Even though the scientists showed them where the landing was, a few days later, when they put the mice back in the same pool, they just swam and swam around the pool in the same way. Then, the scientists took the mice out and injected them with adrenaline. When they put the mice back in the pool, they immediately swam to the platform. The adrenaline helped them remember the dock in the middle of the pool. For people, however, adrenaline doesn't always work out in our favor. For me, the adrenaline reminds me of the pain and causes me not to want to do it again. Most of my anxious feelings are the same. Sometimes the feelings can be more or less intense than other times. They just repeat themselves over and over again. Even if I know it's going to be good and work out fine, my brain makes me think things aren't going to go well, and so I avoid it as much as possible.

Moving in wasn't that bad. The room was old and very dirty. Each layer of the laminate flooring was older and dirtier than the next. With all the heat and grime, it wasn't a good place to be, especially because I'm a germophobe and can't stand dirt and old things.

With little to unpack for a two-week stay, I went with my parents to Johnny Rockets for lunch before they said good-bye to me. I'd been away from home before, but I was always with someone I knew. After lunch, we just said good-bye and walked in opposite directions. I had to go to orientation in a big auditorium to hear people speak about safety. I sat in a back corner of the audience. There were so many teenagers in one place. I always like to sit so I can see most of the place and the exit. It's not something that I'm usually conscious of, but it always happens. I don't like when people can look at me from behind. When I can't see people, I always feel like they are staring at me.

After I sat down, the girl next to me tried to talk to me. She asked me what grade I was in. I told her. After that, I introduced myself and asked her what her name was, but she never responded. I don't know if she didn't hear me or if she was ignoring me, but I was too scared to ask again. So for the rest of the orientation, I didn't try to talk to anyone. I just played on my phone and listened.

Afterward, we had to meet with our RA, Resident Assistant, an upperclassman who lived on the same floor as us. The weird thing was that he didn't even go to the school. He was a college kid who had this job for the summer. The whole floor met, and we played those stupid get-to-know-one-another games. They are always painful for me because I'm supposed to share things about myself with strangers. Even though we are supposed to find similarities with one another, the interactions feel fake. They should just happen naturally. Those are the friendships that really last, not the ones forced. I didn't meet any people that I liked, but maybe I wasn't really open to it.

We went to dinner after the stupid games and talked about policy stuff. I couldn't pull myself together enough to actually order something to eat, so I went to the self-serve cereal machines. I didn't want to tell the person behind the counter what I wanted. I didn't want to be with all the other kids. When *it* gets bad, I'm not always hungry. When I get that feeling, I can keep myself from eating for a long time.

That night, I complained to my parents that I wanted to come home. They persisted in convincing me to stay there. That night was so hot. I stayed in my room and watched *ER*, my favorite TV show, on my iPad. I called my aunt and told her that I was fine. Winston Churchill said, "If you're going through hell, keep going," but this hell felt too big. I'm embarrassed to say that; who am I to say that I was "going through hell"? Other people have a lot more problems than I do, or they go through a lot worse things. What the fuck do I have to be so upset about? (Or to even write a whole fucking book about?) It could always be worse. Always.

My class was in the middle of the day. I wasn't able to go to the cafeteria to get breakfast because I didn't know how to get there and because it wasn't air conditioned like my dorm room. I just kept making excuses to myself. I stayed in my room, watching *ER*, and talked to my parents. Eventually, I did get hungry. I went looking for someplace to go near my class. I was walking in circles. I became really frustrated and anxious. Finally, I saw a Chipotle, but when I walked in and saw that I'd have to tell the kid what I wanted, I walked out. I really wasn't in the mood to talk to anyone.

I kept walking. I didn't go in any specific direction; I was just walking. Eventually, I found a convenience store. I bought an iced tea but nothing to eat and walked back toward my class. Even though class wasn't for another hour, I went because I had nowhere else to go. I found a walkway between two buildings across from where I had class. I sat on a ledge in the shade and cried. I couldn't hold it back. That was one of the first times I'd cried in a long time, and the last time I remember crying.

Nowadays, I can't get myself to cry about anything. I try, but it never works. Funny thing was that while I was sitting there crying, a tour group walked by, and all I could hear was the tour guide telling the prospective parents and students how great Nicholas University was. I'm not sure if they noticed me. I tried to turn away.

When I called my parents the next time, they knew that I'd had enough. Luckily for me, my mom was supposed to be laid off at the end of the week. She took off the rest of the week and planned to stay with me at my brother's apartment, which was twenty minutes away from school. By the time she arrived, I'd already had class, which made it a little better. It made me not want to go home, but I knew I didn't want to stay there by myself. I felt so alone and helpless. There's a huge difference between feeling alone and being alone.

After class, I went back to my room, packed my things, and watched *ER* until my mom came. Just before she got there, someone knocked on my door. The RA and another student asked me if I wanted to go to the cafeteria for dinner with them. I told them no and then told the RA I was leaving.

After this kind of thing happens, I always feel like I have failed. I look at what opportunities came up that I didn't take, like when they asked me to go to dinner. Or when kids come up to talk to me, and I just answer whatever question they ask and never ask any questions back. But it's always easier to think about what I could've done than to think about changing what I will do the next time it happens. By thinking about it, I get better at noticing those times in the moment instead of after they happen.

The rest of the experience was relatively uneventful. My mom found out she wasn't getting laid off, so she had to go back home. My grandparents came up for the second week to stay at my brother's apartment, and every day they drove me to school and picked me up after class.

I actually enjoyed the content of the class. It was called "Technology and Its Effects on Business and World Economies." The teacher was especially nice and seemed to know a lot. For class, I learned that I had to give a mini-group presentation and a final presentation. We were allowed to do the final presentation as a group, but I chose to do mine by myself. The final presentation wasn't hard, but for the mini presentation, we had one class to prepare, and when it was time to present, I couldn't connect my computer to the projector. The other kid in my group talked while I tried to fix the connection. I blocked out what was going on, and I fixed the connection. I had no idea what he had talked about. I didn't want to repeat what he said, so I didn't say much. All the kids were looking at me, waiting for me to say something. I said a few words and sat down. I don't know what happened. I didn't pay attention for the rest of the class. I was in my own world, getting angry at myself and at *it*. I wanted to punch myself in the face.

Every day after my grandparents drove me to class, they'd do something for two hours until it was time to pick me up. My dad's parents really like to go shopping, but they never buy anything. Everywhere we go, they'll find some junk store or department store. They walk around and 99 percent of the time they never buy anything. I don't understand it, but who am I to judge the way they do things?

During the first weekend, we went to the mall to see the Batman movie, *The Dark Knight Rises*. I got really nervous because I didn't want to see anyone from the program who might know me. I didn't want anyone to see me with my grandparents, going to watch a movie, while they were with friends they'd made and having a good time. Still, I often enjoyed spending time with my grandparents. My grandfather is very funny. In my family, we usually find our own jokes funny. It's a very dry, stupid sense of humor. But I find just about everything he says hysterical. As I'm writing this, I'm laughing because of how stupid-silly it is. I really like hanging out with them because I'm laughing half the time. There's something different about being with people my own age, but I didn't spend any time with kids my own age outside of the class.

We arrived at the movie early and found seats. Ten minutes later, seven kids from my class came in and sat right in front of us. I felt like I was dying. I'm pretty sure they didn't notice me when they came in, but they saw me when I left with my grandparents. Of course, what I didn't want to happen did happen.

This was just around the time of the movie theater shooting in Colorado. Some guy shot people at the movie during one of the big shooting scenes. A lot of the people heard the shots but thought it was from the movie. I was already on high alert about seeing people, and with the remote possibility of what happened in Colorado happening here, I was a wreck inside. I couldn't concentrate on the movie. I spent more time watching other people in the theater than watching the movie.

After that weekend, we didn't go out much. I just wanted to go home. I finished the week in class and counted the days until it was over, and I could go home. My presentation was on electric aircraft, and it actually went well, but I just wanted to get out of there and never go back.

Chapter 17

It's Time to Make Some Theater

After getting involved in the video production club, Kevin asked if I wanted to help with the tech for the musical. He liked me, and I liked him, his humor, his creativity, and his confidence. No matter what the problem was he could always fix it. He was very handy.

He mentioned that he needed someone to operate a projector. I was hesitant, but he was very persistent—he kept bringing it up for a few weeks. I finally agreed, but it was some time before I heard anything else about it.

A few weeks later, he mentioned it again because it was Tech Week at school, which was very special at MDS. More than half of the kids were involved in the school play in some way, and with a high school of only sixty kids, they needed about the same number of kids helping to produce the show as were in the show— just about everyone was involved.

I didn't know the plays were a big deal. I knew we had a lot of them, but I never went to them or heard much about them. In public school, plays were a thing that the weird kids did.

My job was to work the projector backstage. There was a fifteen-foot ladder behind the stage with a projector on top of it, facing a small projection screen hidden in the set. At specific times throughout the play, I had to project a video or a picture onto the screen. My job was to switch the images from the computer to the screen when they needed to be there.

Energy is different when doing theater. The only way to understand is to be part of a show. The suspense and practice and aura of all of it is just fantastic. Ever since my first show,

Urinetown, I have been addicted to doing tech. It's mainly a show about a water shortage and a repressive government. Eventually the people rebel and a bunch of stuff happens. It was a pretty good show, from what I heard. I was always backstage, so I never saw any of the show. I only heard what was going on.

Working on the show was fun. This was the first time I saw kids outside school hours. During Tech Week, I was with them from eight in the morning, when school started, until after rehearsal, which didn't end until eight to ten o'clock at night. This was also the first time I realized how much I liked keeping busy, maybe because I had no time to think or feel, or maybe because it made life go by faster. It's hard to think about wanting time to vanish, but I did. It's not that I didn't want to live. It's just that I didn't want *it* to happen.

Working on the play was fun and made me feel more comfortable at school. I made a lot of new friends. Not that I didn't know the kids before, but now I talked to them more often. The kid who did the lights was graduating the following year, so I volunteered to do lights when they couldn't find anyone else. I didn't know what I was getting myself into. For the four performances of *Urinetown*, I had always been back stage, running the projector.

The next year I learned a lot from Shawn, who was a year older than me and had been doing the lights for the shows for a while. I learned a lot about lights, colors, and even some physics, which was very cool. I liked having a "job" at school and the responsibility for me to be at a lot of the school events. Otherwise, I would never have gone to them. Shawn was very nice, and we talked a lot when we were doing shows, but during school I always felt awkward talking to him. He wasn't one to initiate conversation, and when I did, it always made me uncomfortable. All in all, he really showed me what it was like to be friends with other people. I was jealous of him because of how many kids came up to him, especially girls. Everyone in the school knew him as being a genius, and he kind of was.

Getting to know other kids took time, but once I got to know them, and they got to know me, it was a cathartic release. Sooner or later, I became really friendly with a lot of kids. Study hall was a great place to talk to kids because no one, besides me, really did work. One of my study halls only had two kids—just Andrea and me. She would try to talk to me while I was working on homework, and eventually I looked forward to it. I loved it when people talked to me and asked questions.

By the time junior year came around, a lot of kids in my grade had left, including Lucia and Anya. I was shocked to see all the new people. We had about ten new international students from China in my grade. We also had a new girl from the UK. Her name was Grace, and she had golden blonde hair. It was also the last year of high school for Shawn and a bunch of seniors with whom I had become "friends."

The first day of homeroom Andrea came up to me, which made me really happy. We were both shocked by all the new kids. The new girl was very pretty, but she didn't seem too happy to be there, and I couldn't pull myself together to say hello. My first period class was AP European History with Mr. Anthony. The room was set up with six blue rectangle tables in a U-shape. I sat at the far side of the room on the end so I could see everyone else and the door. Grace sat across from me, on the other side by the door. She had a weird English-Scottish-American accent that at first annoyed me, but I started to like it after a few days. She and Andrea had become good friends by the second half of the year, and I eventually talked to her when Andrea was also there.

Chapter 18

Constitutionality

I joined the debate team in my junior year because I wanted to practice public speaking. I felt like it was something I needed to do. My mom said I was good at arguing. I liked thinking and talking about issues, and a few other kids at school also said I should try. People had asked me to join the year before, but I had dismissed the idea. Or I should say *it* dismissed the idea. My first year, I didn't debate. I watched and listened to learn as much as I could from the other kids on the team. Mr. Anthony was the debate coach, which I was excited about because he was my favorite teacher, and he really knew what he was doing. He was a very good presenter in class and it seemed like he knew how to talk really well. Only a few schools in the county were in the competition. Every year, there were two debate meets at hosting schools and then a third match, depending on if your team made it to the finals. Each school had two teams of two kids. During a match, each team competed four times, twice as the affirmative and twice as the negative. Each debate lasted about forty-five minutes. It was a lot of talking for a day.

I was the main researcher on the team. We all did research, but it was my only job. I tried to give feedback whenever I could during practices, but I didn't think I had anything useful to say. The resolve for the first year was, "The federal government should enact substantial legislation to combat the obesity epidemic." Our job was to create an argument for both sides: one that agreed with the resolve and came up with a plan to solve it; one that disagreed with the resolve, stating that the status quo was good enough. I had fun with it, but it seemed so fake to me. The arguing, the judging—all of it, especially because each judge seemed to grade the debates differently. We also weren't allowed to use the Constitution as a basis for argument in any of the debates. There didn't seem to be a unified concept. I thought my opinion of the judges was fairly objective, but because I was in the competition, it might have been frustration. It just seemed like a game that we needed to learn to play, but the rules were contrived in such a way that I didn't understand. That year we won four out of sixteen debates. It was the first time for all of us at this competition. I was the only junior, so it was fun to hang out with some of the seniors and learn from them.

The next year I was the only kid still in debate from the previous year. Mr. Anthony and I had to recruit new kids. I thought two of the guys in the grade below would have made an unstoppable team, but they both said they didn't want to join. Some other kids joined, but to me, we didn't feel like the prior year's team. The year's resolve was that the "United States should substantially revise its gun laws." I told Mr. Anthony that I would debate if I had to but that if we had enough kids who were interested, I wouldn't. I really did want to, but I made excuses.

The other kids who eventually stuck with debating were Max, David, Lea, and Ivan. Max was only in eighth grade, David was a sophomore, and Lea and Ivan were juniors. I was the only senior. A few other kids stayed with the team to do research on and off. Ava helped out too. It was good she came to the debate meets. That year, our first meet didn't go well—we only won once. The debates were at another school, and we had to be there at eight in the morning, so I drove straight from my house. I offered to drive Ava because she only lived five minutes away from me. I had driven to her house only one other time, when I drove her home from musical rehearsal one night during Tech Week.

I picked her up at 7:30 a.m., and we listened to the music I had on my phone. She didn't like some of it, until John Mayer came on. We listened to "Free Falling" and "Waiting on the World to Change." They both seemed fitting. By that time, we'd arrived at the meet. We waited for everyone else to get there. I brought folders with a bunch of paper and the print-outs of the speeches for all the kids debating.

The debates went the same as the year before. Some judges said one thing, and then, for the next round, a different judge said the complete opposite. Ava made me laugh with the things she said, which weren't always very nice. After the debate, we had to go back to MDS because school wasn't dismissed yet. Ava asked me if we could go back to her house first so she could change; she was staying after school for band and thought it would be awkward to be at school in her nice clothes.

"We need to ask Mr. Anthony first," I told her, "because we'll show up after everyone else, and he won't have known where we were."

"You ask him," she told me. "I don't want to. I think he likes you more so there's a better chance of his saying yes."

I tried to get her to ask, but Ava is very good at getting people to do things for her. She's pretty good at making me feel guilty, which is something that amazes me. I eventually did ask, and he said yes.

When we stopped by Ava's house so she could change, I decided to change there as well—I'd brought clothes with me—because I was uncomfortable in my suit.

I told her, "I'll go in only if no one is home. I would feel awkward going into your house to change in the bathroom." I don't know why I was scared of going in her house; it would've only been her mom anyway, and I knew her. She was always at the school performances, helping out with costumes and stuff. She wasn't home, though, so I went in with Ava through the garage. Her house was messier than I expected but nice. We went up the steps from the basement. She showed me her cat, Ringo, and made me pet her, even though I told her I was allergic to cats. Luckily, nothing happened. Ringo was a tiny white cat with black patches. She was nicer than all the other cats I've been near.

"Where's the bathroom?" I asked.

"Around the corner past the kitchen," she said. As she showed me, we passed by the refrigerator, and I stopped because it was covered with magnets and photos. I saw pictures of Ava and her sisters when they were little. A black square magnet with white letters read, "*Life begins at the end of your comfort zone*—Neale Donald Walsh." I smiled at that and took a picture of it with my phone. Ava then pointed me to the bathroom and went upstairs to change.

I realized that her house was the first friend's house I had gone to in at least ten years. Before that, when I was in preschool, my mom made a couple of play dates for me with other kids. I thought about that a lot for the rest of the week. I was both happy and sad about it, though I didn't tell Ava. On some level, I think she knew. But maybe she didn't.

We had two weeks to prepare for the second round of debates. We reworked our material based on what we'd learned at the last meet. We spent a lot of time working on it, practicing, and rearranging the teams.

I picked up Ava to go to the second meet, and when she got in my car, she said Ivan was sick. I brushed it off, thinking it wasn't a big deal. "Find out whether he's coming or not," I said. By the time we pulled into the parking lot, she'd received a text from him saying he wasn't coming. I knew that meant I would have to debate, but I didn't want to think about it.

"Do you think Mr. Anthony s going to ask me?" Ava asked.

"Probably," I told her, "if I tell him no." That meant I had to say yes because Ava didn't want to debate.

The day before in statistics class, Andrea and Grace asked if they could come to the debate. "We've never seen you in a suit before," they said. They were excited about it. I didn't understand why, but it was nice of them. Girls seem to get excited about the strangest, littlest things sometimes.

"You probably can go," I said, "but you'll have to ask Mr. Anthony."

When we got there, I still wasn't sure if they were coming, and then they arrived with the rest of the team.

Mr. Anthony walked right up to tell me that Ivan was not coming. "What do you think about debating?" he asked.

I said, "I'm not sure."

"Take a few minutes to think about it, but I need to know soon."

I nodded, and then told him I would do it. I didn't even think about it. I had never done a practice debate, but I had watched eight the year before and four this year; plus, I'd watched our countless practice debates. I actually felt pretty good about it in a prepared sort of way, though not so much in a "feeling good" sort of way

The debaters from all the schools were in the library, the "home base." I was used to seeing all the kids because it was my fourth debate meet. By the time the rest of our team arrived, we were late, and the only available table was in the back corner. We put our stuff down. They were beginning to call out pairs of schools for the first debate. I thought I would have time to sit and calm myself down, but as soon as we got there, the ball started rolling. I just wanted it to be over already. It's crazy how the end always seems so far away while it's happening, but once it's over, it seems like it only took three seconds.

Mr. Anthony called Andrea and Grace over to the side. When they came back, I asked what they'd talked about. I assumed it was about me. They said nothing. I think Mr. Anthony told them to go to the debates I went to and to sit in the audience so I could look at them. At first I wasn't sure if having them there would make me feel better or worse because they'd be watching me.

Mr. Anthony didn't have to judge the first debate, so he watched mine. I also wasn't sure if that was a good thing or a bad thing. Having strangers judge me was one thing, but having people I knew watch was completely different. The school bell had rung, and we were walking down the crowded hallways that were encased in lockers to get to the room for our debate. It brought me back to my middle-school days. Mr. Anthony tried to give me a pep talk and told me to look at him, Andrea, and Grace. "If you need to, just follow the script. You can do this," he said.

Surprisingly, I wasn't that nervous, but I was shaking a little. As we walked into the classroom, my right hand was shaking, and I grabbed it with my left hand. It was like a cold shiver that I felt on the inside, which also made me clamp my jaw down. After the first side gave their opening argument, I went up to the podium. I was shaking, but as I got into it, the tremors drifted away. It was just my facts and me. I kept looking from Mr. Anthony to Andrea to Grace, which made it look like I was trying to make eye contact with the room. The girl who I was going against in the first debate was pretty bitchy. She kept giving me eye rolls and randomly raising her voice or cutting me off. It was actually rather frustrating. I couldn't help but laugh at Andrea's reactions to the things the girl said and when she raised her voice at me. Andrea's eyes widened and I saw her with a shocked look on her face.

At the end of the debate, I was convinced we were going to lose because I was laughing at the other team, and the judge would say that I wasn't being "professional." We happened to lose, but the judge never said anything about my laughing. But the team remembered my reaction, and it was something to laugh about. Andrea and Grace also wanted to kill the girl for yelling at me.

The rest of the day was much the same. David and I won only one match, but the experience for me was what mattered. I proved to myself I could do it. During one of the matches, the judge had to remind us to settle down because we were getting heated during the cross-questioning. He saw I was frustrated with the other kid. I looked at the judge, and he waved his hands, trying to tell me to calm down. We didn't make it to the third round, but I don't think anyone expected us to.

After the debate was over, we drove back to school. I went straight to Cindy's desk to sign out. She sat at the main desk in the children's school. People always went to her if they needed anything or to just talk. She was very motherly to everyone. Most of the team was already there, telling her how I had debated and almost yelled at some kids and how some bitchy girl yelled at me. They were all happy and excited about it. It was strange that they were happy that I'd yelled at someone, but I kind of understood why. These were stories that we had together

Chapter 19

Better Yet?

After narrowing down my college search, I found two small schools in the Boston area that focused on business. I was looking for a school that had a pre-college summer program so I could see how it felt. I needed a second trial run to prove to myself that being away at school wasn't the end of the world. Since the first time seemed like a failure, this one needed to be great.

I knew that there might be some problems, but this time I knew I could do certain things, so it wouldn't be horrifically overwhelming. I was older, "wiser," and I had some "new rules." Of course, the ride to school was pretty bad. Whenever I go to one of these things, when I get out of the car, I get all stiff, like I was just sitting on an airplane for fifteen hours. But I can't let *it* win, and I force myself to go.

We walked over to the building where we had to check in. Just before I got there, I stopped and told my mom I wanted to go home.

"You can't," she said. "It's only five days. How bad could it be?"

I knew that leaving wasn't a possibility, but I'm always looking for immediate relief. I needed someone to tell me that leaving wasn't a possibility.

We walked into the dorm where I would stay. The bottom floor was one big common room with a giant conference table, a few couches, and a TV. All the kids who had already checked in and unpacked were sitting on the couches, using their phones and watching TV. They weren't talking to each other. When someone walked in the door, the all turned to look at the person and then turned back to their phones. It felt almost robotic and orchestrated. A woman running the program was sitting at a table with a bunch of papers and a computer. I went up to her and told her my name, but I spoke too quietly and had to repeat it. After she found my name, she gave me my key. My parents and I signed forms that said I wouldn't do anything that I wasn't supposed to do, and if I did, it wouldn't be the school's fault.

After I got my key, I went back to the car to get my suitcase and brought it into the building. The kids still were watching everyone else come in with their parents and their stuff. I found my room—in a suite on the third floor. A bunch of kids had already moved into the suite and were sitting on the couches. There were two double rooms, one single room, a bathroom, a kitchen, and a living room with two couches. One of the kids introduced himself to my dad, which I thought was kind of creepy. I said hello to everyone, and they told me their names, and I told them mine. It was very awkward and quiet. My parents and I walked down the hallway and found my room. We went in, and I asked them to close the door. I put the air-conditioning on because it was way too hot for my standards. I stood there for a moment and closed my eyes, trying to calm down. My parents knew what was happening, so they too just stood there and stayed quiet.

I started to unpack my stuff, and my mom made my bed. After I finished, I took another break and sat in the desk chair. I again said, "I want to go home." When I was calm enough, we walked out of my room and left the suite. We walked downstairs, and my dad asked the staff if there was anything else we needed to do. They said no, and we went outside and walked slowly to the car so I could say good-bye without dying of a panic attack in front of everyone.

I don't like hugging people, and I didn't hug my parents. I often flinched when people tried to touch me—no matter the person; no matter the occasion. We just said good-bye. I can't remember the last time I gave my mom or dad a hug. It makes me anxious just thinking about it. After they left, I went back inside and found a seat near the door in the common room with all the other people. I sat there like everyone else and did stuff on my phone. Keeping busy helps to drown *it* out. It's all about distraction. I watched as other kids checked in and interacted with their parents. The kids sat there and played on their phones, watched TV, and talked. Everyone waited for everyone else to come in. The room slowly filled up, and as more people came in, more people started talking to one another. I just sat there.

That day we did "icebreakers"—the stuff I hate about these stupid college programs. They made us play games. A bunch of the guys went outside to play soccer in the field in front of the building. We all had to go outside. We couldn't be alone. I sat on the grass under a tree. The guys played "shirts vs. skins," which made me even more uncomfortable. I tried to just focus on the ground, playing with the grass. The one good thing was that no one bothered me about not doing anything, which was actually a first. One kid had a boot splint on his foot, so he also sat on the grass, and another kid came over. We talked a little, mostly about college, GPAs, and other random things that seemed foolish. One kid was talking and laughing about his six-point-something GPA. I just kept quiet because no one really cared. At least I didn't.

The other days were a little better because we had class. The college has a makeshift trading room that they are overly proud of, and some of the teachers came there to talk to us. The program was Wall Street 101, and they spoke about stocks and bonds and what-not. A lot of kids didn't understand what was going on, even though I had figured they'd know a lot because they signed up for the program.

I had been investing with my dad since I was ten years old, and the lectures were about the stuff he and I talked about all the time. I liked talking about work with him. In the computer room, they did trading simulations that were at first kind of fun, but it was really just a few kids taking advantage of the other kids who didn't know what they were doing. It was all really fake—I mean, really fake.

I also didn't like living with the other kids. They stayed up late and were very noisy. I felt like I didn't have any of my own time. The mornings were the worst because I was so scared of getting ready in the morning and that someone would see me. I got up really early to make sure I would be alone. The bathroom was set up so the toilet was in its own room with a door, the shower was also in its own room, and then there were two sinks in the area between them. This area was open to the hallway and the rest of the suite. My expectation that someone would walk past while I was brushing my teeth or shaving killed me every morning. I was exhausted by the time I was dressed and ready. I brought my clothes and a towel into the room with the shower. Some of the other kids walked around the suite in a towel, and it freaked me out and made me uncomfortable. I shaved at the kitchen sink because it was around the corner, and the chances that I would see another kid were much slimmer. I heard some of the other kids go into the shower while I was in the kitchen, shaving.

Every morning I would count down the days, and as I was getting ready, I would tell myself, "The worst is almost over." It ended up not being that terrible, and I never did see anyone else. But in the moment, I felt I couldn't handle it.

We went on two company visits to see what working in finance was like. I couldn't see myself doing it, ever. Some of the kids were very fake. I'm not sure if they were lying to us or lying to themselves or both. I kept saying to them in my head, *"Stop trying so hard."* Andrea sometimes called me an overachiever in school, but I couldn't imagine myself being like these kids. One of the kids went around telling others that their nametags were on the wrong side of their shirts. At that point, I just wanted to leave, not from being uncomfortable but from being done with people.

At the end of the program we were put into groups and had to give a mini-presentation on two stocks. It was fine because I didn't know anyone, and it was the last time I was going to see these people. Parents were invited to the presentations, another one of those things where the school was trying to show off to the parents. I told my mom and dad not to come; they protested, but were okay with it. There was also supposed to be a lunch, but I told my parents that as soon as my presentation was over, I wanted to get out of there.

I later learned that my dad had arranged with the person who ran the program to videotape my presentation so that he and my mom would still get to see it. I didn't find out he'd done that until a couple of years later. I still haven't seen the video.

Chapter 20

Are You Alive?

Are you alive, I mean really *alive*? I know I'm not sure that I'm real. Do you feel like you are present in the world, and the world is present in you? There were a few moments at MDS when I finally was able to say yes to that question. The moments were different but also were exactly the same. They were times when I felt like I belonged somewhere and like I was at home. Since then, I've never thought of home in the same way. Home doesn't need to be where you live; it's where you feel present and alive—not just that you are physically present but that you really *feel* it. I still only feel that way when I think about my time at MDS and when I go back to visit. Some of that is probably just my memory tricking me into feeling nostalgic. Sometimes, though, it really was true, not just an illusion.

Chapter 21

What Do You Mean?

One day when I stayed a little late for lighting, I sat waiting in the gym on the wooden bleachers looking at stuff on my phone. Grace was there late too for some reason and I saw her walk through the double doors coming from the children's school. I smiled and excitedly waved to her. She smiled back and walked across the gym to me. I'm not sure how we got to the topic, but we started talking about prom and the party that usually happens afterwards. I told her I would go this year because it was my last chance. She seemed kind of surprised. It was more of a pleasant surprise than anything else. She then said something to the extent of, "You may be better off not coming." I didn't really say anything, but I felt a knot in my stomach. I quickly steered the conversation to something else and a few minutes later we said goodbye for the day and she left. I stayed there waiting on the bleachers for a minute just not moving. I got up and turned off all the lighting equipment and walked to my car.

I wanted to just forget about the whole thing. But I couldn't stop thinking about what she said. I made myself text her that night.

Me:

Grace: Put the quote in your book.

Me: It's already been up on the bulletin board for a month. I sent it to you because you told me I would feel uncomfortable going to after-prom.

Grace: You would be uncomfortable because there will be alcohol and possibly other things. And it's not so much you being uncomfortable; it's us being awkward.

Me: Okay.

Grace: You're still invited. I didn't mean it in a bad way, like I don't want you to come. I was just saying it because I know you don't like that stuff.

Me: Okay, thanks.

Grace: I feel bad. Don't think you're not invited.

Me: Please don't feel bad. I understand that you were just looking out for me as a friend. The past few months have made me rethink who I am. For my entire life, I've lived on the sidelines. I'm tired of being the kid who doesn't do anything. Going to Starbucks with you was the first time I'd ever been somewhere with someone from school outside of school. After the first debate, I went to Ava's house because she had to change clothes before we went back to school. That was the first time I'd been to a friend's house since I was six, when my mom made my play dates. I've never been to a party. I've never had a girlfriend. Please don't think I'm telling you these things because I'm mad at you. I just want you to understand where I'm coming from. I wouldn't be telling you any of this stuff if I didn't think we were close enough to be honest with each other.

Grace: I understand what you are saying, but don't come just to prove something to yourself or to me—or anyone for that matter—or to just write about it in your book. Come because you genuinely want to and will have a good time. And I am glad I was your first.

Me: I want to come to prove to myself that I'm me, and that I can have a good time doing things that may be uncomfortable for me now but don't have to be. And when am I ever going to get the chance again to go to a high school party? I'm glad too.

Grace: But are you going to have a good time if you're uncomfortable? And trust me; high school parties are not all that kids say they are. I'm not trying to get you not to go. I just want you to be sure you know what you're getting yourself into

Me: Okay, thanks for looking out for me.

I was so angry at her when we were having this conversation.

Chapter 22

The Little Things

In February of my senior year, I applied for a full academic scholarship to another college. I had to write an essay on what I was passionate about. I wrote about mental health and this book. I wrote that I wanted to do something to reduce the stigma of mental health issues in society.

They invited me to come for an interview weekend, when all the top choices would compete. Of course, I wasn't interested in going, but I was motivated enough to force myself to go. Whatever money my dad saved for me that I didn't use for school, he said I could keep. Making $170,000 for a weekend didn't seem so bad.

In the end, if all I got was three days at the college I'd probably be attending, it would be worth the experience. Probably. We were told to arrive in business attire. That made *it* that much more difficult because I hate wearing a suit and getting dressed up. I get so uncomfortable. I would wear dark jeans and a black T-shirt every day if I could.

When we got there, as soon as my mom turned off the car, I told her I wanted to go home. She got out of the car, walked around to the passenger side, and waited. I waited inside the car. She knew what was happening, and so did I. After a minute or two, I got out and closed the door.

I was very self-conscious to be carrying my suitcase with me. No one told me what to do with it, so I just put it down in the parking lot. My mom told me to bring it, but I wouldn't. I put it back in the car. I was almost at my limit, and with a long weekend ahead of me, that wouldn't be good. So we walked to the Student Center and up the steps to the meeting room, where a few rooms connected to each other. There weren't a lot of people, but the space was small so it felt crowded. I had to check in and receive all my information. My mom found information about what she was supposed to do. After that, we were supposed to "mingle." Mingling and I don't mix. We received a photo roster with our welcome pack, and I noticed someone familiar from the previous summer program I was at. I got along well with her there, so this made it a little more bearable.

When we were waiting outside the meeting room, a woman walked up to my mom, and they both said that the other looked familiar. The woman then realized they owned the house next to our summer house. The woman's granddaughter was here as well. I didn't know her, but she wasn't completely a stranger. My anxiety went down a little and made it a little more bearable. This time, the people I "knew" (but didn't know) made me feel better.

I also met the host, with whom I would be staying for the next two nights. He was a first-year who had won the full scholarship the year before. We exchanged numbers so we could find each other later. He seemed really nice, and we planned to drive my bag over to his dorm that night when my mom left. Leaving my bag behind turned out to be a good idea. My dad had arranged with the school that I would only be with one other person since I couldn't have my own room. We made sure I also didn't have to use a communal bathroom and that I had access to a bathroom with a lock.

When the parents went off to do their own thing, all the kids went into the larger meeting room. There was food, but I couldn't eat anything because I was too anxious. I told everyone who asked that I had eaten before I got there, which was true but also was an excuse for me and for them. One girl came up to talk to me; I think it was because she saw I was by myself, off to the side. I had nothing to say. But I did feel better that she came to talk to me. I felt like I was being less awkward.

They had us go into another room with about fifty chairs set up in a circle. We said our names, where we were from, and what we'd had for breakfast. All the really important things. Then the president of the school came to schmooze up to us, and the dean came to talk. Then we just jumped right into it, and they had us do a bunch of activities. There were hawks all around the room, watching us and taking notes. I don't know how anyone could've acted normal in that situation. We had to talk about ourselves and do this project and a bunch of other nonsense. We also had a one-on-one interview, which I enjoyed and believed meant something.

That night we attended a dinner with all the kids and parents. There were a few hundred people in a cramped auditorium. My host met me there, and we talked a little. He tried to talk to me about flying. He asked too many questions, and I had been done for the day for a while, so I was in no mood. I didn't want my mom there either. I just sat there and tried to stay as calm as I could. A bunch of people from the school spoke, but only the dean actually said something that stuck. What he said was probably the biggest reason for me to go to the college.

During his speech he talked a lot about taking action and about our responsibility as people. He said, "We all have the responsibility to leave the world better than we've found it." When he said this, something really clicked. I felt good listening to his speech, but once I remembered where I was, it all went away. When the dinner was over, my host brought me back to his room, and I brought my luggage there and said good-bye to my mom. I changed out of my suit, and he took me to the theater. We had tickets to see the school's production of *Chicago*, during which I fell asleep. I went outside to the lobby, where it was bright, and I didn't have to spend as much effort trying to keep myself awake. I didn't know where I was going, and I didn't have a key to the room, even if I could have found my way back. So I just sat there and waited for my host to come back. Before the show, he'd told me he was going to study for his test the next day.

One of the older girls from the previous year's competition was walking past the theater and must have recognized me from earlier in the day, so she came in to try to talk to me. I didn't say much. My host eventually came back to the theater, and I was relieved to be able to go to sleep. He had a purple air mattress for me to sleep on. With it blown up and my suitcase on the floor, there was little room to walk around. He told me he was probably going "out" and asked if I wanted to come. I told him no. He offered me a beer that he had in his fridge, which freaked me out. I just wanted to sleep.

I put my headphones on and fell asleep quickly. I woke up a few times from music outside the room and kids yelling. There must have been a party in one of the next rooms. I heard some drunk kid barge into the room while I was sleeping, and I heard my host pull him out and tell him not to go into the room. I immediately went back to sleep.

I woke up from my alarm, which I had set to go off early. I grabbed my clothes and towel and walked out of the room, hoping that I wouldn't see anyone and that I wouldn't get lost. My host had showed me the bathrooms the day before, but the place was confusing, with a lot of hallways. There were two single-use bathrooms, each with a toilet, shower, sink, and a door lock. There was a larger communal bathroom with stalls of showers, sinks, and toilets. I found the hallway with the two bathrooms, and both of the doors were open. I went in one, closed the door, and double-checked the lock. I went to the sink and saw that it was filled with vomit. I got sick to my stomach with a wave of emotion. I picked up my stuff and went to the other bathroom, but it was exactly the same. I laughed that of course this had to happen.

I went to look at the communal bathroom, which was just around the corner, walked back out, looked up and down the hallway, went back into the second private bathroom, and just stayed there. I wanted to sit there and cry to myself, but I couldn't. I cleaned up the sink with paper towels, soap, and water. I pulled myself together and got ready. I didn't say anything when I went back to my host's room. He was already up.

"Good morning," he said. "I hope we didn't make too much noise last night."

I told him, "No, it was fine."

He left to get ready and then brought me over to the same place as the day before. We were watched again as we went through more nonsense activities.

That night, we went to a Boston Celtics game. I hated it. It was too bright and too loud, and there were too many people cramped in the place. I didn't understand how, if there were an emergency, we could all survive. We went back to campus, and they made us stay up to talk to the older kids from the school, without any faculty present. The whole weekend was exhaustion on top of exhaustion. I don't know how I didn't pass out. Even though it felt like torture, it was a nice place, and there were a lot of interesting people.

Chapter 23

Are You There?

Grace was curious, so she asked me if I ever felt something like "awkward silence," or if I didn't get it because I was quiet, and it was natural. She also asked if I didn't talk because I didn't want to or if I didn't have anything to say.

I realized that people don't know what I mean when I say I can't talk. I always assumed that others could understand *it*, but I don't know why I believed that. The only way I could describe it was that I couldn't talk. None of it was under my control. My body just wouldn't let me. Strange to think about it now—that my body could convince me that I couldn't do it. I don't know how it's possible. And I went through it. I can't imagine what others think.

Chapter 24

Every Show Must End

My senior year was tough because I knew high school was almost over. Just at the time when I felt like I belonged, felt like I was home, it was ending. This year I was the top person when it came to lights and tech stuff. During my sophomore and junior years, I'd worked with someone who knew more than I did, so I could ask for help. This year, I was that person. I was the one responsible. I think this was the first time I was in charge of something. I was scared, but I liked the challenge and the responsibility—most of the time.

I recruited two other guys to train—one freshman, Colin; and one sophomore, Joseph. Colin was new to MDS and had done lights at his old school. It was good to have someone who knew about the stuff, but he was used to much newer equipment. He was very helpful with everything. Joseph was also very helpful, but sometimes he just tried too hard. He would talk too much and ask too many questions, and he just annoyed me. The year before, he liked to watch Shawn and me do lights, and he would come up to the lighting booth sometimes. I yelled at him once to go back down because he was too annoying. This year, because of how much work and time was needed at certain times of the year, I thought the more kids who were interested, the better. I knew it would be tough for just one person to handle all of it, even though I had done it on my own a lot of the time—Shawn had started acting in the shows during my junior year and didn't do lights as much. Ji-Woo did spotlights for the shows, and we got to know each other pretty well. She was very bossy. Ji-Woo and I became closer from being in a lot of the same classes. I used to help her a lot with biology and chemistry because those subjects were my favorites.

Each year, the school put on one drama in the fall and one musical in the spring. Kids, parents, alumni, and even parents of alumni would come to help build the sets and make costumes. Judy and Kevin pulled off amazing productions without a lot of resources from the school. Over the years, I grew really close to them. They were almost like grandparents to me by the time I graduated.

That year the drama was *A Christmas Carol*. It was my first time doing a show alone. The first thing I did was watch a production online to get a feel for the show and the mood. Mood may be the most important element in lighting design. I met with Kevin to discuss what he wanted to do with the stage. MDS didn't have a lot of space; our gym was our auditorium and cafeteria. Twice a year, we built the stage and knocked down the stage. The lights were never in the same place two years in a row, never mind two shows in a row in the same year. For each show, we had to change every light. For the big shows, we had forty to fifty lights. And once the stage was set, we couldn't go back up and fix them because the Genie lift we used to reach the ceiling couldn't go on the stage, and the stage was under some of the lights.

We always had to guess where the stage would be. Kevin was pretty good at giving us directions, but he also looked to make things bigger and better, which led to more work for us. Sometimes, it also led to our telling him no, which was tough, considering we too wanted to make the show the best it could be. MDS just didn't have the resources. This, though, made us all pretty resourceful.

It was strange teaching other kids what I was doing, partly because I don't really like to teach, but also because I didn't know 100 percent what I was doing. I was learning as it happened. It goes against almost every bone in my body to say this, but sometimes you just have to pretend like you know what you're doing and hold on. That's how I felt at the time. Joseph, Colin, and I spent hours getting everything ready for Tech Week, the week before the show. The weekend before, I went in by myself with Judy and Kevin and did "dry tech"—we went through the show without actors and programmed the lights to the computer. We worked until midnight. I enjoyed doing the lights. I enjoyed being at MDS. I enjoyed being with Judy and Kevin. They were very good at letting me know how much they appreciated my help, which definitely worked on me.

Tech Week was *always* a cluster-fuck. Getting all the pieces to work together was really difficult, and people either came late or left early or forgot some of their lines or missed their entrance. People were always scrambling for something. Miraculously, though, the shows were always good. The show always went on. The process taught me a lot about trust and how people can surprise you and rise to the challenge. It boggles my mind that it always worked out. Some of my favorite parts of Tech Week were when we ate dinner together; I hung out after school with a lot of people who I liked. I was always busy.

Ava routinely came up to the lighting booth to spend time with me. At first I thought she was coming up because she felt bad for me being up there alone, but we became really good friends. I waited for her to come up. Each time the ladder creaked, I knew someone was coming up. Sometimes it was other techies, but soon I could tell who was coming by the noise the ladder made. The techies ran up the ladder with purpose. But when the ladder only creaked a bit, I knew it was Ava. She was like a cat in how she could sneak up on me. Sometimes I was wrong when I listened, but I always hoped to be right. She was also amazing on stage. No matter what role she played, she was passionate about it, even though she often told me she hated it.

Most of Tech Week, I was busy on the shows. Programming, focusing, and setting up was *a lot* of work. Lights had to be fixed, re-fixed, and changed again. During the fall drama, I became comfortable with the system, even though it was twenty years out of date. It was always short-circuiting, and the old stuff wasn't compatible with new equipment. For the spring musical, we had a new lighting board, which I had to learn to use because the software was nothing like the old one. It was new but not easier. Now I really didn't know what I was doing, and I had to teach other people.

At the end of each show, the seniors who took part in the production would give flowers to people who helped out. We gave Judy a charm for her charm bracelet. This time, because there weren't many seniors in the show, juniors also stood on stage to thank Judy. They asked me if I wanted to take part, but I couldn't pull myself to do it. I got really frustrated because at the last show in the fall, I'd told myself that I would do it in the spring. I wanted to tell Judy and Kevin how much I enjoyed working with them and how much MDS meant to me. But I was too scared. Scared of what, you might ask? I don't really know.

Chapter 25

My First

During the spring of my senior year, Grace kept bugging me to go out to lunch with her or to Starbucks after school—we both finished classes early most days—but I always said no. We had a bunch of classes together and also ran the school store during recess. We were together a lot during the day. I loved hanging out with her at school.

But one Thursday, after seventh period, we drove to Starbucks. She went in her car, and I went in mine. Starbucks was only a few minutes away from school. As I drove there, I was really excited. I was smiling big and laughed every now and then. I had jokingly asked her on Tuesday when we were going to Starbucks. Actually, I was serious, but I had that tone that could've seemed like a joke if she said no. I knew she wasn't going to refuse, but I was afraid.

I followed Grace's car. She drove a gray VW Bug, which I really liked. It was a very cute car. I drove a black Nissan Juke, which other people thought was a cute car. In the parking lot, she pulled into the last spot on the right side. I pulled in next to her. My eyes felt like they were shaking inside my head, like they were shivering in their sockets. I peeked at myself in the rearview mirror to make sure I was okay and to look at my eyes to tell myself I was okay. She got out. I sat there for a moment and then turned off the car and got out. She asked me why I was moving so slowly. I didn't answer, and we walked together to the entrance. For a Starbucks, it was small but had a large outside patio. I followed her in, and she got on line.

Something happened at that moment that I can't truly explain. I felt like we became unhinged from the world and were in this other space, set on top of reality. Grace seemed so fake to me. She was just standing there, looking pretty with her blonde hair down and wearing dark sunglasses. I think my brain didn't believe what it was seeing. In that moment, I realized it was the first time I was ever outside of school with a friend. I had never gone anywhere with someone from school to do anything. This was surreal. It made me sad to think about. All that time, I'd missed out on going places with other kids. All the experiences I'd missed haunted me.

I told Grace I had to go to the bathroom. I walked into the bathroom and stood in front of the mirror, looking myself in the eye to get me to "wake up." It helped, and I went out and found her waiting for me with her drink by the register. We went outside to sit down. We stayed and talked, not about anything specific really but just as friends. I felt present in my world, and I was happy about that.

Chapter 26

Pursuit of Happiness

A better title for this chapter might be "Pursuit of Normality," because I think that's what I was really chasing. Not that I wasn't chasing happiness, but it wasn't true happiness. It's just what I thought happiness was supposed to look like. I finally *chose* to chase it two weeks before I graduated at the end of May.

Prom day was anxiety hell. I felt like everything was going to go badly—like death was imminent, and my chest was going to explode, and demons were going to come out and eat my dead corpse, and even though I was dead, I would still feel it.

I felt that way, and that is what mattered in the moment. I always laugh when people tell me to simply think that nothing will go wrong—as if I didn't think to do that! It didn't matter what I thought about something; it was only how my mind reacted. When my mind thinks that something is threatening, that's how I'm going to feel, no matter what someone else may think about the situation.

No one can tell you that your own explanations of your feelings are over the top. People can't take your feelings from you or say they understand what it means to be you. The feelings are yours and yours only. Who's to say someone's feeling of oncoming destruction is more or less real than the next person's? If you feel it, it's as real as it needs to be. It needs no justification to prove your reality to you or anyone else. Fear is justification in itself, no matter how irrational the fear may seem to others or even to you.

It didn't help that most of my friends didn't show up to school that day because the school policy was that if you were going to prom, you could leave at noon. We were supposed to have the entire day off, but because of making up snow days, they took it away from us. Most kids decided to stay home anyway. If I stayed home, all I'd think about was *it*. By being busy in school, *it* would go away a little, or so I thought.

I went to school, but I wasn't busy doing anything, and none of my friends was there. The other mistake was that I continued writing this book to pass the time, but that just made *it* worse. I sat in the corner of the library for the entire day, worrying. It didn't help that I was having a bad couple of days anyway. I couldn't blame my friends for not being there. They had stuff to do to get ready for prom. I was happy for them because they were able to be happy and excited for prom.

I just kept hoping they would show up, even though I knew they weren't coming. I know this might sound selfish, but it was real. I just wanted a friend at school to help me through *it*. I was in a constant state of threat evaluation.

For week, kids had been talking about prom and what they were going to do after prom. Over the years, I'd heard stories about how this person got drunk, or this kid "hooked up" with that kid. For some reason, I had a hard time believing this stuff because everyone at MDS seemed so innocent. In tenth grade, after hearing such stories, I learned a lot about people. During lunch, I used to sit in a certain room at school to do my homework. There was one desk in the corner and a big table in the center of the room. I usually did my homework in the corner, and sometimes kids would come from the cafeteria and sit there and talk. They knew I was there studying, but they would talk anyway. I listened to them talk about kids as I did my homework. I hate gossip, and I couldn't believe that at such a small school, kids still talked about one another, even kids who I thought were best friends.

After prom, there was usually a party at a kid's house. Because the school was so small, ninth- through twelfth-graders could go to prom. I never went to prom, so I was never invited to the parties. But I heard the stories and decided that this year I wanted to go. I at least wanted to go to one party in high school and hang out with kids outside of school. I didn't want that regret to hang over me, with all the others, for the rest of my life. People started asking me to go even before they knew where the party was going to be. I said yes. It was strange because I usually never said yes to their invitations to anything out of school.

On the day of prom, after I had what was the worst day in a while, I went to my writing advisor, Dr. Albright, to discuss my senior project. But it was canceled again. It was fine with me, and it seemed fair because I had given her the things we were going to talk about only the day before, and she didn't have time to look through it. Because I was doing something so personal with my project, I made sure to pick a mentor who I was close to and was comfortable talking to. My main advisor, Ms. Rivera, was also my homeroom teacher for ninth and tenth grade, and we became close. She was originally from Spain but moved to France, and she could speak a bunch of languages. She tried to get me to practice my Spanish with her and made me speak only Spanish to her when I could. She was very strict sometimes, but it seemed more genuine for some reason. She was always trying to push people to do their best.

When I went back to talk to Ms. Rivera about what was happening with my writing advisor, she became angry about all the meeting cancelations. Then I got angry because I wasn't in the mood, and I was having a bad day as it was. After a few minutes of reprimanding me, she stopped. She must have seen it in my face, because she asked me what was wrong.

It was around 2:00 p.m., and *it* was progressively getting worse—almost as if the dominos were going down one by one, getting closer to something. So I said quietly, "I'm nervous about tonight."

She stopped talking about my project and tried to calm me down. She didn't help much, but it helped me to know that someone was trying to help. She asked me questions about prom and told me to just keep telling myself, *I'm going to be okay.*

"Are you taking anyone to prom?" Ms. Rivera asked

"No," I resigned

She asked, "Why not?"

"I don't want to," I told her

"Are Andrea and Grace going with anyone?" she asked

"Most people are going alone," I said.

She said, "Do you want to take anyone?"

I said, "No"

That wasn't quite the truth, but I couldn't force myself to ask anyone. I also didn't want to make anyone upset. Originally, I thought of possibly asking a close family friend that I had known my whole life, but I thought it would be too awkward for both of us. I don't dance, so we would have been sitting there doing nothing. She wouldn't have felt comfortable with all of those strangers. I didn't think it would be good for either of us if I asked her, no matter how much I wanted to go.

My next thought was of taking someone from school, but I wasn't sure if I would be able to stay the entire time. I might have such a panic attack that I wouldn't be able to go at all. And I would feel really bad for the person I was supposed to go with. I also wouldn't have been able to decide who to ask from school. I didn't want to make anyone upset. It was like a maze inside my head, and I was trying to find my way out. I just made the decision to not make a decision and to go alone.

I didn't tell Ms. Rivera any of that, though. I just told her I wanted to go by myself. After our conversation, I drove around and listened to music to calm down.

I just sit and listen to that one song that makes it all fade away, and my body runs on autopilot. I don't think about anything. It's the best feeling in the world, and it always helps. It's just like when you are listening to a song in your headphones, and you have it just loud enough to tune out the rest of the world. And it's like you don't exist for that split second. It's like you can pretend that you are the person in the song, and you feel your hand tap to the beat, and it all starts to fade away. You watch people walking by, and you try to figure out what's going on, what happened to those people today, who they are going to be in ten years, and what happened to them ten years ago that made them the way they are today.

When I came home, I walked straight to my room, put my headphones on, and went to sleep. I wanted to make *it* go away. In my sleep, I can't feel anything. Sleep is the only time I really can get rid of *it*. Otherwise, *it* is always there. Always.

I slept for three hours, but it felt like only seconds. I wanted time to stop. I didn't want to have to go, but deep down I knew I wanted to go for the experience. That's why I forced myself to get up and dressed. When else would I get the chance to go to my senior prom?

After putting on my suit, I stayed in my room for thirty minutes, just staring at my bedroom ceiling. I wore a dark gray suit with light gray pinstripes. It was more fitted than most of the clothes I wore. It came with a vest too. The back of the vest was a shiny red fabric. The same fabric was on the inside of the suit jacket. I wore a black shirt, black tie, and black shoes with it.

I couldn't leave my room. I sat on my bed, trying to think about nothing, but I was thinking about everything. I knew I should leave my room and do something to get my mind off prom. I walked down the hallway and sat at the kitchen counter. I was anxious, sitting there, because my mom usually made a big deal out of these things. Some of the worst times are when I'm with my family, which doesn't make any sense. But when has any of this made sense?

I talked to my dad about how long it would take me to drive there. I worried there would be a lot of traffic because it was a Friday night of a holiday weekend. I left forty-five minutes before prom was supposed to start. I couldn't stop checking my phone, hoping for a text message from someone—anyone. I wanted to know I wasn't "alone." Before I left, I asked my friends what time they would be arriving because I wouldn't be able to go in alone. I made sure to talk to them because I was going to have trouble, and they were very supportive. Grace told me they would arrive at seven, when prom was supposed to start.

There was no traffic, which made me less nervous about being late but made me more nervous about being early. I just drove and listened to my music. Some people have stress balls; I have my music.

I had no problem finding the place, which was also good. I parked halfway down the aisle of one of the empty parking lots. I didn't want anyone to see me there early, sitting in my car by myself. I listened to the music from my phone, but I grew tired of it; I'd listened to too much that day. I called my dad, but he was busy. My mom answered, and we talked about random things. I told her I was waiting for my friends and that she shouldn't ask about prom. During the day, I hadn't told her how nervous and bad I was feeling. I could tell she knew, though. Every moment I waited was agonizing. It got so bad at one point that I asked myself, *What are you doing here?* I started my car, but I didn't go anywhere.

At seven o'clock, Grace sent me a text. They were going to be late because they wanted to "look fashionable." I just waited, watching the cars drive by. Every minute felt like an hour, and it started to rain. I was staring out the window, watching the rain, and feeling tense, like a balloon about to pop. It was one of the worst days I'd had in a while—until they got there.

Eventually, I recognized a car but waited to see the kids get out. As soon as I recognized Andrea and Ava, my thoughts went away, and I ran over and stood under Ava's umbrella. They complimented me on my suit, which felt good and helped *it*, which made me feel more comfortable. I told both of them that they looked nice as well. I walked into the hotel with them and, surprisingly, felt good. One minute, I felt like I was going to die, and the next, I felt like it was any other day, even a good day.

We first went into the big room to put our stuff down. Then we walked out to the lobby where the MDS kids were taking pictures. Most people knew that I hate pictures, but I tried to participate as much as I could.

The rest of prom was relatively uneventful. I felt like I had the upper hand on *it* at this point. Kids complained about the DJ because he was one of the students and wasn't so good. He played electronic dance music almost entirely. I didn't get up to dance. That would have been too much. I've never danced, and I knew prom wasn't the place to start. A lot of kids left early. I spent a lot of time talking to Colin and watching everyone else. That was good enough for me. A lot of kids complained about how bad prom was, but I didn't think so. I didn't have anything to compare it to. Plus, I was with the people I loved most in the world. Did it really matter where I was or what I was doing?

The kids I was with wanted to leave, and I followed them. I felt awkward leaving early, but I wanted to continue my pursuit. They were going to Emma's house, so I went too. She was a junior, and I guess she was the only one able to get her parents to agree to a party. Andrea, Grace, Ava, Lea, and Emma were all close. I drove over in my car from the hotel. It was pitch-black out and pouring rain, not a good night to be driving. It was the only time I have ever been scared to drive. I was on the highway, and this time I thought—not just felt but thought—I was going to die. Thankfully, nothing happened. I was the first one there, so I waited in my car again. This would be my first party ever. I just felt like it was happening so late for me. I only had two weeks of high school left. I waited till the last minute. I didn't know what to expect. Most of the kids were sleeping over at Emma's house. I decided that was too much.

We really didn't do much. This was the first time a lot of these kids had seen me outside of school. Kids just talked and then played a game where you hold a cell phone on your forehead with the screen facing out so other kids can give clues about a word that's on the phone, and you have to guess what the word is. Kids tried to get me to do it, but I didn't want to. I just watched. Emma's parents bought Mike's Hard Lemonade for us. One of the kids brought beer. This was the first time I was ever around kids drinking. Kids offered it to me, but I refused. They asked me questions after I refused to drink. People were surprised to hear that I never drank, smoked, or did anything like that and that I had no interest in trying. No one was really drunk, but it was interesting to watch the dynamics.

Early on, when I was sitting by myself on a couch, Grace whispered to the brother of one of the girls who graduated a year before to come talk to me. I know she tried to do it without me hearing, but I heard what she said. After that, he came over and asked me a lot of questions for a long time. I didn't really say much, but I answered most of his questions. I was bored for most of the time. Once Ava and Andrea arrived, I had a lot more fun because they always made me laugh. For the rest of the night, I couldn't stop laughing. I left around one o'clock, which was the latest I'd stayed up in a while, but I felt good. When I left, I said good-bye to kids, and Andrea and Grace walked with me to the door. I said bye to them and gave them both hugs. It was the first time I gave Andrea a hug and the second time I gave Grace a hug. Even though I didn't say much, I think they knew how I felt. And that's all that mattered.

I was starting to feel really good, and when that happens, it never lasts long. I get scared that it's going to go away too quickly, and I don't want it to.

Many times when I was driving to or from school during my last year, my eyes would stay focused on something by the side of the road while I was listening to a song that made me feel like someone understood. Thoughts that it would be easier to just let it all go overwhelmed me. I'd slam my foot on the gas and hear the engine roar as the car sped up toward the side of the road. But

I always turned away. Not even at the last minute. Always well before, because I don't think I really meant it.

By now, you might think I have some things figured out, but I don't. For me, the point is to trying to figure out what the point is. That's what makes me turn away and keep driving on the road. The path that seems like the one of least resistance is hardly ever that path. It may seem like it will make things easier in the moment, but it just makes things worse later on.

Chapter 27

If You Never Try,
You'll Never Know

The Friday before the last actual week of school was Field Day. It was two weeks before graduation, when it still felt like there was time left but also when it felt like I had none at all. The entire school takes part in Field Day, divided into teams of colors. My team was the red team. I didn't want to go, but I knew I would never have the chance again. Andrea and Grace also told me I had to go, which meant that I kind of had to go.

A few weeks before in statistics class, Andrea asked me who my best friend was. This wasn't the first time she asked, but I had never answered—I'd just told her it was my dog, Katie.

This time, though, I said, "How am I supposed to choose?"

She said, "What do you mean?"

I said, "You can't have more than one best friend."

Both Andrea and Grace said, "Aw-w-w," and both agreed that was one of the cutest things I'd ever said. They tried to tell me that I could have more than one best friend, but I was still skeptical about the whole idea.

A few days before Field Day, a list was put up with all the team colors and the names of people on the teams. Each team had a few seniors, who were designated as team captains, and one teacher. I was happy that I got Mr. Felix, my science teacher, who I had for four classes over three years. He knew me very well. I kind of expected that I wasn't going to do anything, but I knew I should go. I arrived early and went to Ms. Rivera's room. She was surprised that I'd come to school, thinking I would've stayed home because I hadn't come in years past. She was the homeroom teacher for half of the juniors. She read the morning announcements, and then we all went outside to the grass area between the buildings. We were the first ones out there, but the field soon started to flood with people. The little kids made me the most uncomfortable, maybe because they were more unpredictable than the older kids. The little kids were yelling and screaming, running to the field, and jumping around when they got there. Teachers told them to stop running and tried to corral them onto the grass. They were so excited. I laughed because of how opposite I felt.

I sat at the picnic table under a tree on the edge of the field. I was relieved to be out of the sun, even though it was still early in the morning and not that hot. Eventually, everyone arrived. Other kids came to sit at the table to get out of the sun. Some were still waking up. It seemed that some of them didn't want to be there either. When they were ready to start, the teachers told us to go stand with our teams. We were all slow to get up.

I wasn't feeling ready. I wanted to get out of there. I tried to get myself to stop thinking. I told myself to listen. I imagined snapping my fingers, telling myself to snap out of it. I had learned this from a TED video I had seen a few days before. It worked a little. The premise was that by using another part of your brain to listen to your surroundings, you distract yourself from the feelings you are having.

The first team activity was to take five minutes to create a chant for our team color. Everyone was yelling and being very loud. I stood to the side, just far enough away so that no one would bother me about it. One by one, the teams presented their chants. I hated it. I stared at the grass beneath my feet the entire time.

Evelyn, the dean of students, told us where to go for the first round. I followed my team and watched. Sometimes, I couldn't watch. For some reason, when I watch people "perform," I get really anxious, and I feel like I'm them. This especially happens when people are on stage. I don't understand because I have no connection with the person. I just stare at the ground when I feel that way to try to make it go away.

The activities made me feel like I was back in elementary school gym class. People kept asking me why I wasn't doing anything. I just wanted them to stop. I wanted to be left alone and for it to be okay for me to just watch. It always seemed like it usually wasn't okay.

A girl on my team, Alyssa, who was nice and didn't ask me too many questions about why I wasn't doing anything, came over. We talked about college, and she asked me what I was doing for my senior project. Most people didn't know what I was doing. Some knew that I was writing a book, but they didn't know what it was about. I didn't have the guts to tell her, so I just said I was writing a book about my childhood. For some reason, she then told me that when she was younger, she had struggled with anxiety. I was surprised because she didn't seem anxious at all. After she told me, I told her my book was about my anxiety.

Later on, she told me that she and some of the other kids changed a keyboard setting on their phones so that whenever they typed "Jesus" on the keypad, the phone autocorrected to "Kohlmeier." She then showed me how it worked on her phone. I didn't really know what to think about it. I laughed, and so did she. I guess I was kind of flattered.

We didn't get to finish our conversation, but before she left she said she hoped to talk with me more. I'm pretty sure she was serious. I'd never talked to another kid who had anxiety. It could've been good for both of us.

That's where it all has to begin—with people sharing their own experiences, with people who can relate and especially with people who can't. Knowing that other people exist who have felt the same as I have, understand what I'm going through, and have come out of it is the reason I'm still here.

Chapter 28

Three Seconds

Senior breakfast was always on the last Wednesday of the school year, the second to last day of school. For this, the school serves breakfast to everyone, and the seniors give small speeches about teachers and other students. We also give people gifts. I spent so much time figuring out what to get teachers and other kids that I was completely frustrated. It's something that I always have trouble with. I wanted to give gifts that meant something and would be remembered, not something that people would throw out and forget. I didn't want to settle.

My mom said I should give people jewelry and gift cards, but those gifts were meaningless. I was into the idea of books. My mom was on the phone with her friend who was a principal of a school in New York City. She said she sometimes likes to give *The Alchemist* by Paulo Coelho, as a gift to teachers who leave the school.

By this time, I was open to anything. I bought the audio book on my phone and finished it that night. I immediately went online and bought eight copies for overnight delivery. I already had decided to give *The Perks of Being a Wallflower* by Stephen Chbosky to Andrea, Grace, and Ava. I looked online, and the one with the cover I liked wasn't sold in the United States. I had bought it a few weeks earlier from Amazon-UK. I also bought Ava five bars of Turkish Delight from the UK because I knew it was one of her favorites. I didn't have a second gift for Andrea and Grace so I told myself that I would wait until I found something more special, even if it was after graduation. (I'm still looking.)

When it was time for the breakfast, I went to the gym and up into the lighting booth. It was partly force of habit, partly to hide and not be on stage, and partly to check on Joseph and Colin, who were doing the lights. But I couldn't hide there for long. Colin and Joseph kicked me out, and Andrea, Grace, and Ji-Woo told me to come down. Another girl, Shira, told me to wait as she went to get my gift—a teddy bear, a cool flashlight, and a really nice card she wrote. She told me to open it there. I was really touched and gave her a hug. Shira was a nice, outgoing girl. She seemed to always be looking out for people, and she always tried to talk to me. She had me teach her a little about the lights before I graduated.

When I was obsessed about getting people "good" gifts, my dad drove me all over the place. We went to a mall in New Jersey, but every store we went into, I thought, *Nope*. I didn't know what I wanted, but I knew what I didn't want, and that seemed to be just about everything. At a small bookstore, I found a sheet-metal airplane kit that I could make. It was perfect because Shira often asked me about flying and if she could come on a flight one day. I always skirted the question.

I spent more than two hours making that stupid metal plane. It wasn't very big, basically fitting in the palm of my hand. I couldn't get the pieces to stick together, so I Krazy Glued it. I put it in a plastic sandwich bag that I blew air into to make it like an airbag, which, surprisingly, worked. Shira thought it was really cool, and because I made it, I thought so too. She told people that I'd made her a plane.

By Monday I was all set, but by Tuesday night, I'd grown more nervous and decided books weren't enough of a gift. I went out and bought Starbucks gift cards for all the teachers. I wrote a message inside the front cover of each book. I also didn't feel too good about my gifts to Andrea, Grace, and Ava. I didn't think it was enough. I wasn't sure if anything would be enough. How could I quantify my feelings in a thing? That was my whole problem.

On Tuesday night I asked my dad to get the gift cards. He kept saying that he was too tired and that he'd already had some wine that night. He told me to go myself. I reluctantly went to the register at Walgreen's with eight twenty-five-dollar gift cards. The woman at the register asked me for my ID to make sure I wasn't using a stolen credit card. I had been there many times before, and they'd never asked for an ID. I laughed a little and moved on.

A few weeks before, I went to Staples with my dad to buy envelopes and sturdier paper for the letter that I was going to write to Andrea, Grace, and Ava. I also bought a present for Mr. Dolan, my math teacher. He often spoke about his awful desk chair. I had sat in it a few weeks earlier during extra help, and it was really bad. The back of the chair tilted forward. I wanted to buy him a new one and asked Andrea and Grace if they wanted to split it with me. They said sure. I sat in almost every chair that Staples had before I picked a normal black faux-leather desk chair, which would be a big improvement. However, I also had to put it together.

At home, I started writing the notes in the books and recruited my mom and grandmother to wrap them in apple-red wrapping paper. I told them not to open the books because I didn't want them to read what I had written. I stuck the gift cards inside the front covers. I didn't know how I was going to tell each gift apart so my grandmother came up with the idea to use small pieces of folded wrapping paper with each teacher's name. I kept a close eye on both my mom and grandmother because I didn't want to get embarrassed because a name was mixed up. I'm sure they've wrapped their fair share of gifts, but that didn't make me less anxious. I was relieved when we finished. I felt satisfied with the gifts. I made sure everything was ready to go before I went to sleep.

The next morning, I woke up earlier than usual and went to school early because I was nervous about sitting onstage to give our senior speeches. I wasn't even going to give a speech, but I didn't want to sit on stage. Seniors had to sit at a U-shaped table on stage. Normally, senior breakfast was outside on the quad between all the buildings, but it was rainy and muddy. I put my stuff in Ms. Rivera's room and went around giving the books to my teachers. I gave Ms. Rivera a book of quotes as well as *The Alchemist*. I told her I wasn't really sure what to get her and that it wasn't enough. Seniors are supposed to get up to the podium, say something, and give their gifts to the teachers. I didn't want to do that, so I gave my gifts out to teachers before the breakfast.

I also went to the mailroom to pick up the T-shirts that Ji-Woo and I bought online. We ordered custom T-shirts that read "MDS Class of 2014," with all our names on the back—all nineteen of us. At the breakfast, I didn't want to get up to say anything, so we planned that Ji-Woo would speak, and I would hand out the shirts.

I didn't eat breakfast. I said I ate at home, which was true. I didn't want to sit on stage, eating, with the lights shining on me. Ji-Woo had moved the nametags so I would be sitting next to her. Whoever put them in place before—probably Evelyn—had Grace, Andrea, and me sitting next to each other, then Blake, then Ji-Woo. Ji-Woo switched Blake's seat and my seat. I kind of wanted to sit between Andrea and Grace, but what could I do? I still could talk to them, so it was okay.

Mr. Anthony said to wait to give gifts to the seniors so the non-seniors could go back to class. We went around the stage, one by one, starting with Grace. She gave gifts to teachers and so on. After finishing with the teachers, she started with me, forgetting what Mr. Anthony said, and gave me a book called *The Geek's Guide to World Domination*. I thought it was pretty cool. I went up to get it and, without even thinking about it, I gave her a hug. All the kids started cheering really loudly and long enough for them to keep going until I sat back down. I guess they all knew that it was unusual for me to do that.

I didn't go up when it was my turn. I felt awkward, but people probably expected it. Ji-Woo was next. She cried handing things out to the teachers, which was okay. Andrea and Grace gave a CD to all the seniors with songs that they'd picked:

1) "How Far We've Come" by Matchbox Twenty
2) "I'll Be There for You" by the Rembrandts
3) "This Is the New Year" by A Great Big World
4) "Keep Your Head Up" by Andy Grammer
5) "This Is What It Feels Like" by Armin van Buuren
6) "Good Life" by One Republic
7) "Don't Forget Where You Belong" by One Direction
8) "I'm Ready" by AJR
9) "Live Like We're Dying" by Kris Allen
10) "Viva La Vida" by Coldplay
11) "Anything Could Happen" by Ellie Goulding
12) "Count on Me" by Bruno Mars
13) "Best Day of My Life" by American Authors
14) "Happy" by Pharrell Williams

Andrea also gave me a book, *The Geek's Guide to Dating*, and a shirt that read "You're my crème de la crème friend." I thought it was hilarious, but only she and I knew that because it was sort of an inside joke. One day during statistics class, we were looking up a synonym for something and "crème de la crème" was one of the ones I read to her, and she just started laughing and kept saying it. I really liked the gift because it was something that would remind me of these years; that was what I thought senior gifts were supposed to be all about. Everyone went up, got hugs, cried, and laughed. I enjoyed myself, even though I was in a partial panic. Kids came and went if they had to go to class, return textbooks, and what-not. I still have all my gifts that I received in my desk drawer at home.

After everyone finished, I told Ava that I had her gift in Ms. Rivera's room. She came with me. Andrea and Grace stayed in the gym, talking to people. Ava was mad at me for not giving her gift during the ceremony. I wasn't sure if she was joking or serious. I gave Andrea, Grace, and Ava a copy of the book and a letter when we got back to the gym. I told them not to open the letter until graduation. I knew it was a long shot, but I still asked.

Back in the gym, we gathered our things, and I asked Andrea and Grace if they were going to the party. They were surprised and asked me what I was talking about. I said, "The Facebook one ... at Shira's house." Both of them were shocked that I'd asked. They asked me if I was going. I said I was going with Ava and asked them again if they were going. They originally said no, then maybe, and, later that night, yes.

I asked them, "Did you ever think I would be the first of us to say yes to going to a party?" Joking, I told them that they had to go, but I was also serious. I couldn't go if they didn't go.

A few days before, when I was making Shira's plane, Ava texted me to ask if I was going to the party. A bunch of people got a Facebook invitation for a "going away" party for the seniors. I was surprised she asked me, but I told her no. She kept trying to convince me, so I told her that I'd go only if she went with me. She gave me an excited yes. After that, I was excited.

After the gift-giving and speeches were over, Ava kept bugging Andrea to go for pizza. A lot of the kids were planning to go. I didn't say anything, but I felt strange because they all do things together sometimes. They asked me once in a while, but I always said no. I didn't blame them for not asking because I always gave the same answer. I liked being asked, though; it made me feel a part of things, I felt bad when I heard about something and I wasn't asked to go. Even if I knew that I wouldn't have gone, and they knew that too, I still felt ashamed. Ava looked over at me and asked in a very friendly voice if I wanted to get pizza with them. No matter how much I wanted to go, I just instinctively said no. I didn't even take three seconds to think about it.

Before I left, Ava told me that Min-Joon, her boyfriend, was going to ask if I could drive him to the party. She told me to tell him no. I laughed and asked why. She told me it would be awkward. I told her I couldn't say no.

She said, "Jon-n-n-n," in her normal annoyed voice. I didn't know why she wanted me to refuse, and I didn't want him to think that I was trying to take his girlfriend from him. When he asked me a few minutes later, I just laughed because I didn't know what to say. Ava was right next to me. She said no, but then I nodded my head yes, and that was that. I went home.

When my parents came home from work, they told me we were going out to dinner with my grandmother. "I want to be home around seven o'clock," I told them. "I'm going out."

I knew they would say okay no matter what, but I was still really nervous. It's much easier to tell my dad things because he doesn't make as big a deal as my mom does. When I tell my mom, she doesn't stop asking questions and talking about it. If I told my dad, he would tell my mom, and I wouldn't have to deal with her. I just told my dad that it was a good-bye party for seniors, which was technically true.

There is just something I don't like about talking to my parents about my friends or things I do both inside and outside of school. It's not about privacy because I couldn't care less if they knew. I just didn't want to tell them. My parents can track where I am on my phone, just like I can track them. Where was I going to go that I didn't want them to know about it? My parents never set any rules about my going out or doing things. They trusted me and, in this case, I trusted myself. My anxiety is a bodyguard. They also just wanted me to be a normal kid, just as much as I wanted to be. They didn't want to keep me from doing things; I did that to myself enough. My mom, especially, tried to get me to do things. I'd always yell at her to stop because I'd had enough of that when I was little. I don't think there's anything wrong with wanting to stay home. The only time it becomes a problem is when you don't want to stay home, and *it* makes you.

We went out to dinner at a new place in town, even though we usually go to the same place whenever we go out for dinner. My mom and grandmother kept asking where I was going and what I was doing. I said, "Even if I told you the person's name, you wouldn't know her or where she lives, so why does it matter?"

My mom said she needed to know where her son was going to be. My dad rolled his eyes.

I said, "You can track me no matter where I am."

Resigned, she said, "You are right."

I just felt like she was being nosy.

When we got home, I put on my usual black shirt and jeans. I had a new quarter-zip from Tommy Bahama from a gift card my dad gave me that he didn't want to use. For the first time in a while, I felt like I looked pretty good. I left to pick up Ava. I had texted her earlier to ask what time I should pick her up, and she told me eight o'clock.

I said, "Isn't the party supposed to start at eight?"

She laughed and said, "Yes, but you're not supposed to arrive on time."

I trusted her because I was new to this.

When I got to her house, I saw a bunch of other cars outside. I texted her that I was there, and she told me they'd be out in a few minutes. I saw Andrea's and Lea's cars. I didn't know what to think. It was kind of the same feeling as before with the pizza. I knew I was overthinking, but it's hard not to sometimes.

They came out a few minutes later. I put on the CD that Andrea and Grace gave me during senior gifts. I really liked it. Ava told me to skip some of the songs because she hated some of them. Ava gave me directions to the house where the Korean exchange students lived. We stopped outside and waited for Min-Joon. After a few minutes, he came out, and Ava was annoyed because he'd made us wait. No one else minded that much. All three cars followed me.

I didn't know where I was going, so I put into my GPS the address Shira put on the Facebook group. It was less than ten minutes away, but I hated people following me or my having to follow people. I didn't want anyone judging me on my driving skills.

Her house was in my town, but I didn't know that area even existed before I went there. I drove up, not having any idea where I was. It was kind of creepy because the address had two houses and a long driveway. We weren't sure at first, but someone pointed at one of the houses, and I pulled in. I parked and sat there with my eyes closed for three seconds, which felt like a long time. I turned the car off, and we got out. I looked at Ava across the roof of my car, and she smiled and laughed. We were on our way.

I walked up to the second house on the lot with Andrea. We saw Shira, who was already a little drunk, and we went in. James, a senior, was sitting on the couch. He was smiling, staring out into nothingness. Someone said he was high. I just kept walking. A bunch of the junior guys, and some other kids who I didn't know were there. I didn't know what to think or feel. I was too stuck to do anything. I just followed. Grace asked if I was okay. It's hard for people to read me, but it seems like just about everyone can tell when I'm in panic mode. It's like I just shut down and am not inside my body anymore. No emotion, no movement.

I just followed Andrea, Grace, and Ava. We went into the kitchen where friends of Ivan and Shira were hanging out. There weren't that many kids at the party, which was good because if there were more, I probably wouldn't have been able to stay. Some panics I can push through, but others I can't. That would've been one I couldn't.

Shira told us that there was beer and margaritas in little cans in the fridge. She told us to take whatever. Shira told us it was her mom's house. It was really nice, kind of old, but recently renovated. The kitchen was really nice, with dark wood and copper. I like architecture, and I liked that this house was in my town, where there aren't a lot of cool houses. I thought the place was cool to see. We went back into the living room. Another guy was acting high, walking around, staring into space. I assumed he was high, but it seemed like he was being overly dramatic. I don't have any experience on the subject, so I assumed that was what was supposed to happen.

Shira was excited we were all there and that I was there. She kept telling people that I made her a plane. And then she told me that she broke it accidentally. She said it broke into a million pieces when she was driving home. She said she was sorry. I guess she also saw that I was kind of in a panic. I kept backing away from her when she moved too close to me. She asked if she was scaring me. I shook my head. Before this, I didn't realize how apparent my panics were.

Shira said the music wasn't working, and she asked if I could fix it because I did tech. I didn't have anything better to do, so I tried. The stereo system was old and big, nearly half my height. It was kind of cool. I didn't know what I was doing, but I kept fiddling with it, turning it off and on again, trying to reset it. After about ten minutes, I got it to work. While I was trying to fix it, someone texted David to bring his portable speaker with him, just in case. Even though I fixed it, we didn't have any good music to play. Someone had the CD from Andrea and Grace, so I put that in. When David came, he used his speaker with his phone and turned off Shira's stereo. I did all that work for nothing, but fixing it had given me something else to think about, and I was in less of a panic. I felt much better.

Kids were drinking and listening to the music. Someone asked Shira if she had red cups or ping-pong balls, but she didn't. Andrea and Lea said that they would go get them, and I went with them for a break. We went in Lea's car, and I sat in the back. At the 7-Eleven, I stayed in the car because I didn't want to bump into anyone, even though practically everyone I was friends with was at the party.

Two minutes later, they got back into the car and made some joke about underage teenagers buying Solo cups. When we got back to the house, Grace and Ava were pretty drunk. I didn't understand how it happened so quickly. Andrea said the same thing to them. We put the cups on the counter, and they began to play a game with two teams, needing to flip the cup over from the edge of the table. I had no idea what was going on. I wasn't paying much attention to the game but more so to the kids yelling at one another.

I saw Lea and Andrea sitting on the steps by the door in the living room. I sat down near them and stayed there for most of the night. When no one was there, I went back into the kitchen and sat there. I wasn't doing much. I talked with the kids who weren't drunk, which was basically just Andrea and Lea. When we were sitting on the steps, I told them I had a question for them. I asked, "Why is this considered fun?"

They just shook their heads and laughed. "It isn't fun," Andrea said. "It's only fun to watch people being drunk and stupid."

Grace came over, and because Grace listens to anything Andrea says when she's drunk, Andrea told Grace to sit down and then stand up. She followed her directions, and we all laughed. Andrea said that was why it was fun. I still didn't get it.

Whenever Grace came over to me, I moved away because I was scared—although I wasn't sure of what. She noticed because she asked, slurring her words, "Am I giving you anxiety?"

As soon as she said that, I felt *it* right through my chest, and then *it* left. I just shook my head. There's nothing worse than someone who knows you have anxiety asking you in public if she is giving you anxiety.

After that, she fell-sat down on the steps with us and put her head on my lap. When she fell, her hand also went on my lap, and I casually moved it because it was too close for comfort. I let her lie there, even though I was uncomfortable. I also felt butterflies because it also felt good.

A minute later, someone suggested ordering pizza, and Grace went back in the kitchen. Lea and I were still talking about life, APs, college, and the future. She's a really good singer, so I asked her if she wanted to pursue that. She told me she didn't think she could make a living from singing. She wanted to go to college in Canada and sing as a hobby. It kind of made me sad because I thought she could make it, but I understood what she meant. This was the first real conversation I had with her over all the years, and it was also kind of the last.

When Lea and I were talking, Shira randomly came over to say she was having a panic attack. I didn't know what to do. I looked at Lea, puzzled, and then told Shira to go outside, which she did. It had been a few weeks earlier when Shira asked me about my senior project and then told me about her anxiety attacks when she was little.

If you make yourself vulnerable to other people, most of the time they'll automatically do the same thing back.

I told Lea I'd be back in a second, and I went outside to find Shira. I thought it was because she was drunk, but I wasn't sure. I told her to take deep breaths and that maybe she shouldn't be drinking. She told me she hadn't had an attack in a while. We waited a few minutes. I went back in, and then she followed a minute later.

Lea wasn't sitting on the steps anymore, so I went into the kitchen and sat on a stool. Grace was talking to some guy, which made me pretty angry because it looked like he was taking advantage of her. He wasn't doing anything specific; I was just worried. He gave me very bad vibes. He started hugging people and tried to hug me. I stepped back. Grace told him to leave me alone, that I didn't like to be hugged. He went to the bathroom. and Grace followed him. I had the urge to stop her, but I didn't. She stopped herself and turned around.

Blake came in a few minutes later. He was smoking this thing, and I had no idea what it was. Lea said it was a vaporizer. I didn't know what it was, but I made my assumptions. What it was vaporizing, I wasn't sure. He also drank some beer. The smoking and the drinking upset me because just a few days earlier, I'd gone to Blake's senior presentation because Shira asked me to go. In his presentation, he talked about addiction, his and others. I missed the beginning so I didn't hear the whole story, but he talked about what it did to him and other kids and how his parents kicked him out of the house and made him go to rehab; he also talked about his recovery. He seemed genuine, talking about it, and I trusted what he said. His parents were there and seemed to believe what he had to say.

Now, here he was smoking and drinking at this party. I felt lied to. I felt bad for him and angry with him at the same time. He said he couldn't have that much because his parents would make him take an alcohol and drug test when he got home. I was livid but didn't show any of it.

All this time, I didn't see Ava. She was roaming around, talking to kids, and I think she went upstairs with Min-Joon. Dong Jin was upstairs too. Shira said he was really drunk and high. He threw up and then went upstairs to sleep. I was worried, and Andrea and Ava went up periodically because they were worried too. When Shira told us what happened, Andrea asked, "Don't you think someone should check to make sure he's not dead?"

Ivan and Emma were in a back room off the kitchen, a part of the house that wasn't renovated. Ava kept wandering in there, and Andrea had to keep going to get her. Ava kept saying that he'd better not hurt Emma. Later on, Ivan came out of the room and went to the bathroom. Some of the guys went up to him, and he washed his hands and stuck up two fingers. I didn't know why he told them because it was none of their business.

Soon after this, I wanted to leave because it was late. I didn't see Andrea anywhere, so I texted her to tell her I wanted to leave. A few minutes later, she came into the kitchen and said she was with Ava. It seemed like she was taking care of everyone and wasn't having fun herself. I gave one good-bye to the group, and Andrea walked me to my car. Ava came outside too, but she stood far away. I gave Ava's house keys, which she left in my car, to Andrea so she could go home with her. I gave Andrea a hug and waved good-bye to Ava.

I plugged my address into the GPS because I wasn't 100 percent sure where I was going. A few minutes after I left, Ava and Grace sent me text messages saying how sorry they were. All I could do was laugh. When I got home, I sat in my car and texted each of them, saying I wasn't mad. Ava said she was a bad friend because she told me she would go to the party with me and then didn't hang out with me. I told them not to worry, that I didn't feel any different about our friendship. I made sure to text Andrea because it seemed like they were kind of freaking out. Andrea told me they were drunk and being paranoid and to ignore them. To get them to stop worrying, I sent them a heart emoji. I didn't have the guts to click on the red one, so I sent them a blue heart. The next day, Andrea told me that Grace showed everyone that I had sent her a heart.

I went inside and walked quietly to my room because I didn't want my parents to know I was just getting home, even though it didn't matter. I didn't want to have to answer any questions about how it went. As I went in, I saw the light from the TV shining under my parents' bedroom door. Maybe they'd fallen asleep with it on, but I think at least one of them stayed up until I was home. I laughed and went into my room. It seemed like it only took three seconds, and I was back to where I had started hours earlier. I had a little trouble falling asleep. When I woke up the next morning, I felt an intense feeling of guilt and didn't understand why. I didn't do anything. But I guess *it* felt different.

Chapter 29

The Worst Things in Life Come Free to Us

All of the seniors were provided a page in the yearbook called "the Senior Will," which sounded kind of morbid to me. Each person is allowed to do whatever they want with their page. Most put pictures of them and their friends or say something like "I give X my spot in study hall" or write something about an inside joke. I didn't know what to write or give people, so I decided to "leave" people songs that reminded me of them. I thought it was a pretty cool way to show my appreciation, rather than writing something cheesy or "willing" people stupid gifts or jokes. I spent hours and hours looking through songs, although I ended up getting most of them from my iTunes library. I had extra space at the bottom of the page, and because I liked the quote wall that I'd made for Ms. Rivera, I put some of my favorite lines on my yearbook page.

As I was putting together the songs, I was texting with Ava, telling her about my idea. She was annoyed that she wasn't getting her own song. I tried to explain, but she didn't get it. I was physically upset and needed to find a way to explain it to her. I wrote the following:

> I've lived my whole life not knowing what friendship really is and what it means to love someone—not loving them in a romantic way but loving them as in caring for that person. You, Andrea, and Grace showed me what that meant, probably not even knowing it. I really can't describe in words how much the three of you mean to me. That's why I couldn't write about you guys in my Senior Will.

You guys are my three favorite people in this universe, and I have never said that to anyone before or about anyone else. I couldn't distinguish between the three of you on a piece of paper. That's why I decided to leave three songs to the three of you that mean a lot to me. Once you hear them, I hope they mean a lot to you too.

After I wrote that I think she understood. After I wrote it, I kind of understood it too. I didn't know where it came from. It was just spontaneous and cathartic. Here are the songs I left for people:

Jonathan Kohlmeier

Andrea, Grace, and Ava—"I Don't Wanna Love Somebody Else," "Shorty Don't Wait," and "This is the New Year" by A Great Big World

Ji-Woo—"Viva la Vida" by Coldplay and "Piano Man" by Billy Joel

Jake—"Good Life" by OneRepublic

Andrew and Alexei—"Young Forever" by Jay-Z

Min-Joon—"How Far We've Come" by Matchbox Twenty

June—"Waiting On the World to Change" by John Mayer

Colin, Joseph, Nick, Max, Luke, and Dan—"Feel Again" by OneRepublic—I know MDS tech can be very frustrating, but if you can develop a passion for it, the frustration won't matter. Always remember the end result of lighting and how beautiful it can be. But most importantly: "mommy and daddy always want to see their kids faces..."

Ms. Rivera, Mr. Anthony, and Dr. Albright—"The Bridge" by Elton John—I can't thank the three of you enough for how much you've helped me over the years.

Everyone else at MDS—"There is an Answer" by A Great Big World

Chapter 30

The Last Day of the Rest of My Life

The day before senior graduation was the last official day of school. Even though classes and exams had been over for a while, we still technically had school for another week. I chose to go in because I knew that I would never have another day of school again, and that scared me. A lot. I didn't think I would find another place like MDS, where I felt like I was at home and where I belonged.

Basically, no kids come to school on this day—only the little kids, and the older kids who procrastinated on giving back their textbooks. It was also a half day. So instead of missing nothing, you were missing half of nothing.

As I was driving, I slowed down going up the long, narrow driveway to soak it all in. I was remembering the things that had happened, were happening, and were going to happen at school. I thought about what I would miss. It was a little before eight o'clock, and I was one of the only seniors. When I pulled into the parking lot, I realized it was the last time I'd be pulling in as a high school student. I didn't have an "I made it" feeling but more of an "it's over" feeling.

I started walking up to the high school building. It was an okay spring morning. There was some sunlight, but as the day passed, it became darker and darker. It fit my mood. I ran up the two flights of stairs, taking the steps two at a time, and went straight to Ms. Rivera's classroom, just like I always did. I knocked on her door and went in after she answered. No one else was there. By eight o'clock, when homeroom started, there were still only a few people. I went to my homeroom across the hall to tell the teacher that I was there. She said, "Hey, Jon!" in her usual high-pitched, excited, but very awkward voice. I said good morning and went back to Ms. Rivera's room. All week, she had me helping to organize her room. Because she was leaving at the end of the year, she had to separate her books and stuff from the school's. I always told her that her room had too much stuff in it. It felt good to throw stuff out, for both of us. We filled up her small trashcan and the recycle bin. Then she asked me to put the stuff out in the hallway so they wouldn't know it was her stuff.

After doing that for a while, she had class with the little kids, which meant I had to go. I went over to the library to kill time while I waited for Andrea and Grace. I didn't get the nervous, panicky feeling I had before prom. I was more excited-nervous because this time I *knew* they were coming. I was waiting for two of my favorite people to come in for the last day of school. Ever. I couldn't have picked better people to share it with.

The night before had been Shira's going-away party for the seniors. I figured Grace might be a little hungover and not feeling so well. I left the library. I waited for them by Cindy's desk. Andrea got there first, and we talked about the night before. Grace came in soon after. Andrea asked Grace, "How do you feel?" in a sarcastic but friendly way. They talked about last night right in front of Cindy, which surprised me, but it didn't seem to matter. I asked both of them again why last night was considered fun, because I still didn't understand.

Andrea repeated that it is fun when you are not drinking to watch other people make asses of themselves. And if you are drinking, it could be fun to be that person. "You have to try things at least once to experience what life throws at you," she said.

We were at Cindy's desk to say hello and good-bye because it was the last time we would see her while we were at school. We knew we would be back to visit, but it wouldn't be the same.

We decided to go around the school and just remember. We started with the tech booth. I needed to say good-bye to my tree house, my home away from home. We went to the gym and then up the ladder to the booth. Grace and Andrea made me go first. When I got up there, I went up to the second floor of the booth, where the spotlights and random equipment were. I looked below at the floor of the gym. I remembered the plays and musicals we did. It was almost as if I could hear the band playing the songs and the kids singing right there in front of me. I saw Kevin's sets illuminated. I saw myself going up in the Genie lift for the first time with Shawn and remembered how nervous I was because the thing always shook.

That all happened in a matter of seconds. I went back down to the first floor of the booth to Andrea and Grace. When I first started doing the lighting, I bought a small six-inch-by-six-inch clear plastic box to store pens, paper, tape, gum, and some other things. I wrote all over the box in black permanent marker, JON K. LIGHTING GYM. GO AWAY. The box smelled of Juicy Fruit. I left the box there. I looked at the lighting board and the names of the people we painted on the wall. I said, "I don't want to go."

Andrea started crying. I turned away because I felt like I was going to cry, and I didn't want them to see me, but it didn't happen. We just waited in silence for a few minutes. We went back down the ladder.

Next, we went back to the children's school, passing by Cindy's desk. Andrea told Cindy I'd made her cry. And I said it again that I didn't want to go, and Andrea told me to stop. We walked down the first floor hallway of the children's school and looked in the four classrooms. I never had any classes in the children's school. Neither did Grace, but Andrea went to MDS for all thirteen years. She told us about teachers and kids who were no longer there. We went downstairs. I'd only been downstairs one or two times in my five years at the school. There were only two classrooms and a door to go outside, which reminded me of the doors at the end of the hallway in elementary school.

We went outside into the rain. Andrea told us about the teacher who kept chickens and that the chickens used to walk around campus. I had no idea how many things about MDS I never knew. I realized there'd be a lot more that happened after I left.

We went back upstairs and over to the middle school building. We did the same thing, just walked around and remembered all the people who weren't there, who had made MDS what it was for each of us. We went downstairs and tried to get into the biology lab, but the door was locked. The lab was one of my favorite places in the school. I was sad that I couldn't get in. I kicked the door and walked down the hallway to the band room. There's a door at the back of the room leading outside, where we had recess in middle school. In the spring, I liked sitting out there and feeling okay just watching kids and talking to whichever teacher was on duty that day. I always liked when Mr. Anthony was on recess duty.

Andrea said that so many things happened for her at MDS. She mentioned her first kiss. Her talking made me sad because I felt so far behind everyone else. The next day, I'd be graduating from high school, and I still didn't have my first kiss. Grace said she couldn't imagine being at MDS for thirteen years and having so much of her life happen in one place. She was only there for two years. We went back inside. Grace went to the bathroom. I told them I'd never seen the girl's bathroom in the middle school. They laughed and said, "It's nothing special."

I stuck my head in because no one else was in the building. They both said that when they used to skip classes, they'd hide out in the bathroom sometimes. I couldn't imagine skipping a class while being in school.

We went upstairs to Mr. Dolan's room and wrote our names in Sharpie on the chair we bought him as our senior gift. We went to the upper school building, passing by the library. My first history class at MDS was in the basement. The room was now a storage room. Surprisingly, the room was unlocked. The room was really different. There used to be one big table and a whiteboard on the wall, with couches off to the side, because it had been the senior lounge. Now there were boxes, old furniture, and some of the international students' suitcases. Some still had the luggage tags on them from China and Korea.

In the back of the room, on the right side, there was a little closet that looked like you could hide a dead body in it because it was all concrete. Andrea was surprised it was unlocked, and she opened it. I never noticed the closet before. She told me kids used to have "parties" in there. The closet could barely fit the three of us, so I don't know what they did. She said they used to play music and put up lights. No one could hear it because of the concrete. I imagined other things kids could have done. Names were written on the walls. I recognized some, but most of them I didn't.

After that, we went outside and walked back to the parking lot. It was raining lightly, and we were kind of quiet. The half day had ended a while ago, and it was almost time for a normal day to end. Andrea and Grace were parked next to each other, and they put their stuff in their cars. I became fascinated by the way Grace's trunk opened. She had a VW Beatle, and the VW symbol opened the trunk. They both laughed at me, which was kind of the usual thing.

I sat down in her trunk because I didn't want to get wet from the drizzle. They laughed, and I said, "I melt and can't get wet." We didn't have much to say or do. We talked about nothing. Andrea asked if she could drive my car. I thought for a few seconds and then said, "Yeah." I told her to stay around the circle driveway at school. I sat at in the backseat, and they sat in the front. Andrea moved the seat and started driving. I was nervous. She went too fast around the circle. Maybe it wasn't that fast, but I didn't really trust anyone, although I kind of trusted Andrea. I would have said no to anyone but Andrea or Grace. (Maybe not Grace.) Andrea came around the circle and pulled into the parking spot next to her car. She asked about the push-to-start key. I showed her my key chains. One said "Bazinga"; my mom bought that because I liked Sheldon on *The Big Bang Theory*. Sometimes we acted similarly. My house key had Bugs Bunny on it. She asked if she could have it. I told her I would give it to her after I moved that week, because I still needed it to get into my house.

That was when she asked, "Isn't your grandfather home to let you in?"

I laughed because I didn't know what to say. I took a deep breath and said, "I never told you guys, but my grandfather died on the Friday of Tech Week. I didn't go to the funeral so I could do the tech for the musical."

They seemed kind of shocked. I felt nervous for them because I wouldn't have wanted to be the friend in this situation.

Grace started crying and said, "I wish you would've told us. I might have been a real bitch to you that week, just messing around. I just didn't know."

Andrea asked, "Do you want to go visit his grave?"

"He was cremated," I answered, "and is sitting above my grandmother's fireplace at our summer house."

She asked me again if I wanted to go, and I said no. To lighten the mood, I said to Grace that at least I got her to cry. She laughed while she was still crying. I told her that I had tissues in the glove compartment. Throughout the day, Andrea cried, I almost did, and Grace never seemed to get close to crying while we were walking around.

After that, we didn't say much. It was getting pretty late in the afternoon. We got out of my car. I gave Andrea and Grace hugs. They both said, "I love you guys." I didn't say anything. Andrea was waiting for me to say it back, but I couldn't.

She asked me if I would say it after graduation. I said I didn't know. She said okay. We each got into our cars and left. Grace went first, then me, then Andrea. Andrea took a picture of our cars lined up and sent it to us afterward.

On the way home, I was wondering why I didn't say "I love you" back. I couldn't remember when I'd said it to anyone, not even my mom or grandmother. I was really mad at myself that I couldn't do it. I didn't understand myself.

When I got home, I sent them this message:

Even though I have a hard time saying it out loud, I want you both to know how much I do love you guys and how much you both mean to me. ❤

Chapter 31
Don't Be Afraid of the Woods

At the end of the school year, MDS hosted an awards ceremony. I was always too scared to go, but this year I went with my parents because the awards usually went to eighth graders and seniors. Each department gave out book awards to an eighth- and a twelfth-grader. When I was in eighth grade, I didn't go because I didn't know it was a big deal, but I happened to win the science award for eighth grade, even though I was at MDS for only half a year.

This time was different because I knew more people, and the ceremony was really for us. I freaked out a little beforehand because I had to get dressed up, my parents would be there, and the kids from school would meet my parents. I kept the two worlds far apart. My mom always got annoyed at me for this. She wanted to be involved and help out. I never let her. She argued with me, but I always got my way in this.

I hate getting dressed up, probably due to my lack of practice. My base anxiety level rises very high, and *it* doesn't let me calm down. But I did it because I had to. I always liked going with the classic black suit, white shirt, black tie, and black shoes. The more inconspicuous the better.

I dressed and was ready to go. I stood staring at myself in the mirror. I saw my panic face and laughed. After a few minutes of staring at myself, feeling like I wanted to die and excited at the same time, I walked out and asked my dad to help me tie my tie. He put it on himself, tied it, took it off, and then I put it on. I always asked him to teach me, but I think he liked doing it for me. Afterward, I went outside and waited in the backseat of my mom's car. I found something comforting about confined spaces.

When I was little and became really anxious or mad, I always looked for places to hide—sometimes under a bed or in a closet. One of the first times that I remember was on New Year's Eve. I was mad at my aunt for some reason, and I ran downstairs to my grandparents' apartment and hid in my grandmother's closet. I heard people calling my name, looking for me, but I stayed there with the light off, curled up in a ball. I must have been seven or eight. I heard everyone running around the house for a good ten minutes. A few times, I heard people walk by the closet door. I didn't move or make noise. When someone eventually opened up the closet and found me, they called my mom over. My mom sat down on the floor and held me while she cried. Then I started to cry.

When I get like that, it's like brick walls are built around me. I'm trapped within myself. I can't remember what happened after that. It's probably better that way.

So I just sat there in the car for a few minutes, thinking about everything and nothing, waiting for my parents. The flashbacks are the worst parts. A few minutes later, my dad came out and then my mom. They know to be careful with what they wear when they are with me, especially at a school event. My mom has an eccentric fashion style—colors and patterns. She knows to tone it down when she is with me. Sometimes not enough for my standards, but sometimes I let it go. Sometimes I don't, and I ask her to change. Sometimes she listens, and sometimes she doesn't.

We left the house early, arrived early, and then sat in the car because there weren't many people there yet. I wanted to wait. The ceremony was at a normal-looking catering hall. It looked like a villa on the outside and was dark on the inside. My dad made a few jokes to lighten the mood, which he was pretty good at, and then we went inside. I didn't wait for them. I was walking like I had a purpose.

I went inside and ignored everyone I saw, other than nodding hello. I saw Ms. Rivera and went over to her. I had seen her a few hours before but was still glad to see her. I really didn't want to be there. She told me she liked my suit, and I quietly said, "Thank you." Ava came in, and I smiled at her. She came straight over to me. The three of us talked and then my parents came in. My heart sank. I had never been at a school event at the same time as my parents. Ms. Rivera saw it in me and told me it was okay. She had worked with me on my senior project and with Spanish over the years, but she had never met my parents. I went over to them with her and introduced her to them. She told them about our work together. I didn't want to hear about it, so I left and went back to Ava, who was standing by herself. Andrea and Grace arrived soon after.

There were a bunch of round tables and one long rectangular table for the seniors in the front of the room, with a podium and a microphone. Even though not too many kids were there yet, I took a seat a few seats from the end. I looked at all the empty chairs. I didn't want to stay. I felt like I needed to leave. But I didn't.

Andrea put her stuff on my left and Grace sat next to her. Some kids saved seats for other kids. Someone's stuff was on my right. A few minutes later, Ji-Woo texted that she was on her way. She told me to save her a seat next to me. I told her someone's stuff was already there. She got kind of angry at me, telling me to tell them to move. I laughed and told her no.

Later, when she arrived, she asked the kid to move down, and he did. A lot of people listened to Ji-Woo. I felt better with her sitting next to me.

The room began to fill up. I grew more nervous and, at the same time, more comfortable in the space. The waiters brought our food to us first. I didn't eat much because I felt like I was being watched. The head of school and the deans said a few words about the class of 2014, and then they started the awards ceremony. The academic dean began with honor roll. I knew she would call me up for that or high honor roll, but I wasn't sure which. Knowing I'd get called up to receive my certificate in front of everyone made *it* pretty bad. She finished calling out people for honor roll, and I anxiously waited for my named to be called. It's like waiting for the dentist to pull your tooth out. Then the dean began with high honor roll. She called my name and some of the anxiety went away. I forced myself to get up and walked toward the podium. I'm pretty sure Andrea physically pushed me out of my seat. I shook Dr. Albright's hand and went back to my seat.

It wasn't that bad, but it didn't get easier as the time went on. That night, I received six awards. Grace and I got an award from New York State that would have given us some money if we were going to a school in New York, but neither of us was. It was still cool for an academic award. I received the History Department book award, the Science Department book award, and the Drama Department book award, all for twelfth grade. My Spanish teacher awarded me the Spanish Department certificate. This was all nice but seemed too much. The best part of the night was hearing Mr. Anthony's, Mr. Felix's, and Judy's speeches about me when they handed me their awards.

Mr. Anthony gave me a biography of John D. Rockefeller and wrote in it, "What makes the makers?" I paused and just looked at it for a few seconds and smiled. Mr. Felix gave me a book about people's relationship to nature called *Last Child in the Woods* by Richard Louv. He wrote in the front cover, "Don't be afraid to get lost in the woods." When Mr. Felix stood up to give his awards, I knew he would call my name. After he gave his awards to the eighth-graders, he started with the Senior Book Award. The first thing he said was, "I've been teaching at this school for three years. I've known who I was going to give this award to for 2 years, 364 days, 23 hours, 59 minutes, and 59 seconds."

Everyone laughed. I smirked because I knew then that he was talking about me. He talked about the four science classes I had with him and that I never missed a homework assignment in any of his classes and aced every test and lab report. He made sure to specify that he grades the AP biology lab reports as if they were written by college sophomores and juniors.

Mr. Felix said, "He has an incredible scientific mind. The way he is able to think about our world, both logically and creatively, is unbelievable. He could be not just a good but a great scientist if he wanted to. But, with all of that, the one thing that really stands out to me about Jon is his character. As intellectual and intelligent as he is, he is such a good person. It's hard to see sometimes because he's so quiet, so reserved." He went on to tell the story of my last class with him and that after class, I went to leave, then stopped, turned to him and said, "This is my last class with you. Ever."

He said, "I know."

I said, "I don't want to leave."

Everyone said "aw-w-w" at his story, which made me more embarrassed, but it was good. He went on to say, "Jon, I know that my being your teacher has meant a lot to you, but you being my student has meant even more to me." When I went to get my certificate, Mr. Felix asked if he could have a hug. I gave him one. Before that, I never really noticed how tall he was, but that didn't matter. I took my award and went back to my seat. Jake put up both hands and made me give him a double high-five, and I did.

MDS has small science classes, which was usually nice. I knew I would miss that. I really liked Mr. Felix as my teacher. In my first class with him, chemistry, he offered to provide me with extra work and to let me use a more advanced textbook for my project than the one everyone else was using.

In between awards, I tried to eat some of the food they gave us, but I mostly just wanted to sit there. I gave my food to Ji-Woo. After that, Judy got up to give awards to kids who worked on the plays. She handed out a bunch of certificates and the book award was last. She presented me with a book on theater tech, a cool handbook for the future. It was called *Fundamentals of Theatrical Design: A Guide to the Basics of Scenic, Costume, and*

Lighting Design by Karen Brewster and Melissa Shafer. In her remarks, Judy said,

> Like a stealth jet, this bright young man would quietly and precisely go about his work, giving directions to his crew with economy, focusing equipment, taking his artistic and technical responsibilities seriously. If he came to me for the trailer key, and I was distracted by six other things, he would politely wait until I noticed him still hovering, his piercing eyes beginning to twinkle. "Keys?" he'd say. Then we'd both laugh. This happened often. Making Jonathan laugh was always a prize.

> He first ran the projections for *Urinetown* in 2012. He was obviously overqualified, but he quickly picked up on the power of collaboration. I think he has always enjoyed working alone, but now he could be part of illuminating art, while staying magically out of the light. "The Kohlmeier," as he was respectfully dubbed, became the one who watched from above, showering brilliant light and color upon our stage.

> Jonathan learned all he could from working with Shawn, as well as a professional lighting designer and an electrician. He taught himself even more. He became brave in dealing with out-of-date equipment, troubleshooting, fixing, and making do. He is also clearly artistic in the use of his technical skills. He is a patient and generous teacher and has thankfully passed his knowledge on to younger students.

> In his junior year, he was co-designer and board operator for *The Man Who Came to Dinner* and *Into*

the Woods. This year, he did the lighting design for *A Christmas Carol* and *Little Shop of Horrors*. He also stepped in to light countless other MDS performances. Kevin says, "Being around Jon was a lesson in generosity. He was not only excellent at his chosen work, but was always there personally, offering a hand."

When we stayed in the gym on the last night of spring break until 1:00 a.m. to set the lighting cues for the entire show, it was like working with a pro. And, yes, he was on time for school the next day.

It has been a great joy to have Jon share his gifts and friendship with us, his fellow students, and with MDS. Jonny, you must now walk into the light! You will be missed by us, but we know you have a bright future.

I knew I was going to miss her and Kevin the most. I loved working with them so much. I went up, and she gave me a hug. She was the only one who called me "Jonny" besides my dad. I didn't really like it when other people said it because it seemed kind of childish, but I never minded when she did. I actually liked it.

I went back to my seat. The ceremony was almost over. I was counting as each teacher went up and sat back down, and there weren't many teachers left to get up. Eventually, they finished the awards. People slowly started to leave. Andrea and Grace made me take some pictures with them. I also took pictures with Ji-Woo and then Jake.

After the ceremony, I went up to Mr. Felix, who was talking to another teacher. When he saw me, he ended the conversation and just looked at me. I didn't know what to say, and I told him so.

"You don't have to say anything," he said. "It's okay. And I'll still see you on graduation. You can tell me then."

I said good night and went back to my seat at the head table. I said bye to Andrea, Grace, and Ava. I texted my parents that they could go outside and wait for me. If they were standing around inside waiting for me, I would have gotten really annoyed.

I felt awkward carrying all the books and certificates. I could barely hold all of them, and it made me anxious. A lot of people said congratulations. It was nice but felt like way too much. I went outside. My parents were waiting in their car. I got in, and we left.

Chapter 32

Nothing Lasts

The next day was graduation. It wasn't until four in the afternoon, but because we didn't practice enough—all the walking, sitting, standing nonsense—the school (aka Cindy) asked us to be there by three. I was there at 2:15.

Surprisingly, I slept until ten that morning, which was very late for me. Intentionally, I didn't do much in the morning. The night before, I made sure to pick out what I was going to wear. What I thought looked good was uncomfortable, and what was comfortable didn't look good, which made me uncomfortable. I had made sure to ask Cindy what to wear. She told me, "Slacks and a shirt," which could've meant a hundred million different things. I asked Andrea because I knew she had been to a lot of MDS graduations. She told me, "Pants and a button-down shirt." That's what I picked out. I didn't have many options and didn't want to wear the same black pants and white shirt, so I wore navy blue suit pants with a blue shirt. These were actually my only choices. I picked the lesser of two evils because I didn't think it was okay to wear the same suit as the day before. The problem was, I didn't like the blue pants. It was too late for me to panic. I knew it wasn't going to help. I hung them on the outside doorknob of my closet, the signal to myself of a final decision.

My head faced my closet while I was sleeping. When I woke up, the first thing I saw was the suit pants hanging from the doorknob. My head fell back onto the pillow. It was in those first few milliseconds of waking up that I didn't remember anything about today, which was good. I could be anyone or anything. But moments like these never lasted. I was back to being me straightaway, and seeing the clothes didn't prolong my unknowingness.

It is just like how I wish I could bottle up the good feelings to remind me of good, when *it* is really bad. Like when it's nice and warm inside, I try to save up as much as I can so when I go out into the cold, I can still feel the warmth. Problem is, no matter how hard I try, I really can't.

Around noon, I ate leftover pasta, showered, and put on the clothes. I had the same staring contest that I had last night with myself before the awards ceremony. I was becoming annoyed at myself. I didn't like the pants because they seemed too long. The shirt was too big and had a giant pocket on the front. After a while, I had to shut the closet door with the mirror on the back because I knew I was making myself sick. I noticed that when I kept my hands in my pockets, the pants didn't seem so big. I also remembered to bring two tissues and a pack of blue Trident gum, which usually made me feel better.

One problem was that it was disgusting outside, with high humidity and a forecast of rain. As soon as I stepped outside, I felt agitated. With rain, my clothes would get wet. I didn't want to carry my wallet and keys in my pants because I'd feel too bulky. I grabbed my rain jacket to put all my stuff in and a tiny umbrella I always carried in my school backpack. The more stuff I had, the more prepared and less anxious I felt.

A few days before, Ji-Woo asked me take her gown to get steamed because Cindy told us to get the wrinkles out. I told her I would because my dad was taking mine, and it wasn't easy for her to go herself because she lived with a host family. Both gowns hung at the bottom of the steps next to the door. I grabbed them as I left. They were a deep forest green. I didn't want to wear the gown because I thought it looked ridiculous. What's the purpose of wearing a cap and gown on graduation? To me, it seemed to be an out-of-date historical tradition.

I hung the gowns up in the backseat of my car. I had my green cap and tassel, with a tacky and unnecessary 2014 gold plastic trinket attached. I plugged my phone into the car and listened to my music to help me calm down. My heart was racing. I felt more anxious excitement than anything else. Something like, "Let's just get this over with already." I didn't really want to graduate, but I knew it was going to happen. I wanted it to be quick, like ripping off a Band-Aid.

At school, I parked my car in the small lot next to the upper school. I didn't see many other cars there. I noticed Cindy's car and a few others scattered across campus. I knew I was early, but I still wanted to see someone. With the air conditioning on, I sat in my car for one song and bottled up as much of the cold air as I could before I went outside. I eventually got out, grabbed the two gowns, and walked down toward the circle to the children's school and the gym. Graduation is usually outside behind the upper school, but because the ground was still wet from rain, and the forecast was for more rain, they set up the chairs and podium in the gym. I walked past the upper school and saw the head of school in her office, talking on the phone. I just kept walking and tried to open the gym door. It was locked, so I went around to the children's school door, opened it, and walked in.

Cindy was setting up boxes of the flowers we were to wear. I hung the gowns, covered in plastic, on the bookshelf next to the door. I had to take my jacket off because I was too hot. I put it on the chair next to the bookshelf. I said hello to Cindy, who was talking to Grandpa Doug, as he was called, who always took pictures of school events and posted them on his website, even though his grandkids had graduated years before. He was always very nice and tried to take pictures of me doing lights during the plays. I tried to hide from the camera. He knew it, and so did I. It was always a pleasure to see him.

I sat in the lobby of the children's school for a few minutes, waiting and talking to Cindy and Grandpa Doug. No one else showed up for a while. I went into the gym. I was surprised by how many chairs were set up. The gym looked larger than usual, but I wasn't sure why. Colin and the music teacher were setting up sound stuff. I said hello and looked around because I knew it was technically my last time there as a student, which I knew was silly to think because I knew I'd be back.

Colin and I were talking, and he gave me a card. I wasn't expecting it, but I was very glad to receive it. As I was opening the card, Colin asked if he could give me a hug. I nodded my head. It didn't happen, though, because the music teacher came back in after changing into a suit and asked Colin to help him with something. I was waiting for him to give me a hug, but it was a relief when the teacher called him over. They went over to the makeshift pit to finish setting up. They jokingly asked if I had any requests. I smirked and said no, but they practiced playing the graduation song. I went back to Cindy's desk to see if anyone had arrived. No one else had come in yet. They started making jokes that no one was going to show up for their own graduation or that they would be late. It made me feel better, though—if no one showed, the nonexistent attention wouldn't be on me.

Eventually, kids did arrive—Jake, then some of the Korean students, then Ji-Woo, then the Chinese students from the dorm. Andrea and Grace came in almost last. One of the Chinese students I was "friends" with, June, came in and saw me in my suit pants and shirt and said in her quiet accent, "Ah, so cute." She made me feel both better and worse at the same time. By the time everyone arrived, we didn't have time to practice. We dressed in our caps and gowns. Andrea helped me pin the white rose to my gown. We took selfies by Cindy's desk, and I felt pretty good. It seemed like everyone else did too. We walked out of the children's school around to the outside door of the gym. Cindy lined us up in alphabetical order.

The other day when we practiced, I was one person off from being able to sit in the second row. I told Ji-Woo I didn't want to sit in the front row, and she told Cindy. I didn't ask her to, but she did anyway. Cindy told me to switch places with Min-Joon. I thanked Cindy and sat in the back row. Getting myself to sit up on stage for graduation was one thing, and making it easier for me by sitting in the back was a good compromise. "If you don't ask, the answer is always no."

I made sure to ask Cindy if she told Mr. Anthony, so he would know that when he spoke about us that we were switched. I was afraid he would call our names in the wrong order. She told me that he knew, but I was still scared. As we started walking into the gym, one by one onto the stage, I saw that there was an extra chair at the end of the row, which would have been for me if Min-Joon and I hadn't switched. I assumed that someone put it there and didn't tell me, so we would sit in the original order. Of course, when Mr. Anthony spoke about each of us individually, he spoke about Ji-Woo, then Min-Joon, then me, even though we were sitting in a different order.

I saw that people noticed, and I didn't know if they thought it was my fault. It didn't matter because I knew I wouldn't have survived up there if I'd had to sit in the front row. If people knew how to spell our last names, they would've seen that we were switched. I was looking at Dr. Albright for much of the graduation because she was one of the only people I could see with the bright stage lights. She noticed when I looked at her, and I watched her turn her head in curiosity when the names were mixed up.

With the class so small, Mr. Anthony spoke at length about some students. I was expecting him to say something profound, but I was surprised he didn't. All he said was, "Jon Kohlmeier. A student. Pilot. Chef. Lighting designer. Friend." He turned to me and said, "Jon, you're awesome. Period. End of statement. End of embarrassment." And everyone laughed.

After sitting down, I noticed Min-Joon's flower was pinned upside down. I debated for ten minutes if I should tell him. I eventually told him, and he fixed it. I figured if we were in switched places, I would've wanted him to tell me.

After just a few minutes of being up there, I felt like I was dying, but surprisingly, not from *it*. I was actually pretty calm, other than the whole seating thing. It was so hot and humid, and the lights were bright, shining on my face, into my eyes. I had never been so hot and sweaty. I literally thought I was going to melt. I thought I was going to pass out from heat stroke. I was surprised everyone lasted the whole time. I barely paid attention to what Mr. Anthony said because all I could think about was the sweat. Eventually, the head of school began handing out the diplomas.

One by one, we went to the front to receive our diplomas. I was too numb to feel anything. Like a robot, I went up, took my diploma, shook hands, and got my picture taken by Grandpa Doug. I went back to my seat, and the worst was over. Finally, it was all over. We left the stage one by one and walked out the same way we came in. We were told to line up outside the gym. All the teachers and other people shook our hands and said congratulations. I didn't know this was going to happen, which was probably for the better. I just went with it. It was cooler outside, and I was the first to remove my cap and gown. My hair was messy, sticking up in the front after being stuck under the cap. I didn't care because at least I was cooler. I tried to fix it and so did Grace, but it just stayed the way it was.

I was glad to see some people, but it felt like a good-bye, and I didn't want it to be. When Ms. Rivera came out, I stepped back from the line and turned around because I thought I was going to cry. It was the closest I came to crying since I was at Nicholas University, three years earlier. After a few seconds, I went back into the line, and we both laughed and gave each other a hug. I was sad I wasn't going to see her so often. She made a big impression on me, and I didn't feel like I could ever thank her enough. She went to talk to my parents, and I followed. She kept saying nice things about me. She was crying in front of them. We looked at each other and laughed.

It turned out that after I left them, my mom begged Ms. Rivera for a copy of my book. She originally said no, but she later sent it to her in an e-mail. My dad spilled the beans one night when we were driving home from dinner. I wasn't angry at either of them. I was kind of glad she'd sent it to them because I knew that I wouldn't have been able to.

I went back inside to speak with Judy and Kevin. Joseph and Colin were turning everything off, and just before they did, Joseph pointed to the dimmers and asked me, "Would you like to do the honors?" I went in and flicked the three switches for the last time. Back outside, I gave a few other teachers hugs and handshakes. Colin came up to me, and I reached out and gave him a hug and told him I would be back. I gave Ava, Andrea, and Grace hugs too. We took pictures, and it all felt right for once.

Soon after, we all went back inside because it started to drizzle, and we had to give our caps and gowns back to Cindy. I kept my flower and tassel, though. I saw Mr. Felix inside, and I quietly said hi. He congratulated me, and I gave him a hug.

He said, "Have you figured out what you wanted to say?"

"No," I said, and I laughed.

"I know what you meant to say," he told me, which was probably true. That was the last time I saw him.

I followed Andrea and Grace into one of the classrooms in the children's school to return our caps and gowns. We looked at one another and hugged. I had to back up and turn around because I felt like I was going to cry, which both of them were. I wasn't as close to crying as I was before with Ms. Rivera, but I still came pretty close. A bunch of us stayed there for a while, saying good-bye. It was pouring, and kids started leaving as it got worse. Grace and I were the last to go. Andrea had to meet her family. I grabbed my umbrella and stuff and walked Grace to her car. We both got soaked, even though I had the umbrella. Her parents had left the flowers they brought her on the front of her car. They were drenched. I told her to get in. I put the flowers on the passenger seat and closed her door after she got in.

I ran to my car, got in, heard the door shut, drove home, and then it was over. I didn't feel that sad, which was surprising. I was worried that I was going to have a real breakdown. Like I wasn't going to be able to function. Like I wouldn't be able to speak.

This was the letter I wrote to Andrea, Grace and Ava, the one I told them to open after graduation.

Friday June 13, 2014

Dear Andrea, Grace, and Ava

I'm writing you this letter because I want to make sure you know how much the three of you mean to me as friends. To be honest, you three are the only real friends I've ever had in school and I want to make sure you know how special you guys are to me. I've lived my whole life not knowing what friendship really is like and what it means to love someone. Not loving them in a romantic way, but loving them as in caring for that person. The three of you have shown me what that truly means, probably not really even knowing what you were doing. I really can't describe in words how much the three of you mean to me. You guys are my three favorite people in the world and I'm really going to miss not seeing you every day. I don't know how I'm going to survive school without the three of you. Whenever I was having bad days I would always think of going to school and getting to see the three of you. Having that to look forward to every day always made me feel better.

I can't thank the three of you enough for helping me get through all those things that were difficult for me. Now that we are not going to see each other every day at school, I really don't know what I'm going to do with myself. I wanted to write this letter to you because I never told you guys how much you mean to me and I didn't want to leave MDS without you knowing that. It's hard for me to talk about my feelings out loud and I didn't want you guys to feel that I didn't appreciate our friendship. I really hope that we get the chance to stay in touch after we graduate and that we will all still be friends when we are fifty years old and will remember our years in high school together. I wanted to give you "The Perks of Being a Wallflower" because it helped me get through some bad times and I think every teenager should read it. The book means a lot to me and I hope that it will mean a lot to you too. I hope that it may help you one day when you are going through some bad times and that you will think of this and you will think of all the people who love you.

THANK YOU.

Love Always,
Jon

Part 4
Quintessence of Dust

This was the bridge that I was on with my mom when I tried to jump out of the car. I took this picture during one of my first solo flights.

Chapter 33

Absolutely Nothing

Have you ever noticed that other people are real? I know this sounds like a stupid question, but think about it. Other people actually exist. They have their own thoughts and feelings and problems. Isn't that strange? And we have no idea what actually happens to them when we're not there. But a lot of the times, we think we do.

I remember the first time I realized this. I haven't thought the same way since. It was my junior year of high school. It was winter, and it had snowed the previous night or that morning. It was Monday's morning meeting for the upper school. Teachers gave their usual announcements about what was going on. At each morning meeting, a different teacher would speak on a theme, usually referencing famous quotes or things that were supposed to make us think more deeply. I really liked this part of the day. Mr. Anthony was normally the go-to person when other teachers didn't have anything to say.

Mr. Anthony told us a story of when he was at camp, and all the kids were sitting in a circle, talking. He said one girl started talking about really bad things that happened to her. He said she had a rough life with her parents. When he heard these stories from other kids his age, Mr. Anthony told us that it suddenly clicked for him that kids have struggles, and he had absolutely no idea who went through what or what happened that morning to that kid. Maybe she was hit by her parents every morning, he said, or maybe they died in a car accident. The point was that no one knows anything about anyone.

After he told us about this, he said, "Other people are real... Other people are real." He was good at saying things dramatically. He then waited. He was very good at reading people. He said that his life was never the same after realizing this, and having heard him, my life hasn't been the same either.

Chapter 34

Unable to Stay,
Unwilling to Leave

Think about *it* as getting stabbed in the hand by a knife each time you talk to someone or meet someone new or do anything where you might be watched. Most of the time, I know I'm not being watched, but even the remote possibility of it is exaggerated by my brain. Even when I'm in my room with the shade open, the .00001 percent chance that someone is going to see me puts me on high alert, and I can't focus on anything but the knife that's stabbing me. It slowly goes through me as if to deliberately make it more painful. I know that most of the time I will get stabbed, so it is not a surprise. That's probably the worst part; I know *it*'s coming so I try to avoid *it*, but when I can't, I just worry about how bad *it*'s going to be this time. I try to build up enough strength to avoid the knife. But it takes time ...

Jonathan **Kohlmeier**

A lot of time ...

...

to learn how to play the game.

And even when you thought you knew how to play the game or that you have finished playing, the rules change, and it starts over. So it gets really hard to ignore *it*, and it's really easy just to keep yourself from situations where you know that you're going to get stabbed. But then you don't live your life because you let the fear rule your life.

And that's when I get depressed. After building up enough strength to attempt to ignore *it* during my senior year, I couldn't explain how much better I felt. I got to the point where I could get numb to *it* sometimes. It allowed me to really connect with some people. And it's a part of the human experience that is unlike any other. It makes me feel like I am really alive, and I get to feel how powerful friendship and love really are.

Chapter 35

Smarter than We Are?

March 13, 2014

As I write this, I am a senior in high school. I don't know why you might think I am writing this, and to tell you the truth, I'm not 100 percent sure myself. Partly, it's to tell people my story so others can understand *it*. But I don't think that's the whole part.

The name of this entry is my reaction to an interview with the author Russell Banks that we read in English class. In the interview, he says, "There is a wonderful intelligence to the unconscious. It's always smarter than we are." When I read this, I immediately thought of how untrue it is for people with anxiety. My unconscious tells me how bad being social is by bringing me pain and torture. How could that possibly be smarter than I am? I'm not bashing Russell Banks or what he said; it's just that what he said in this interview really got me thinking. How complex does *it* have to be to manipulate me and make me scared of one of the most basic things in life, one of those things that makes being human, human?

My having lived with anxiety for my whole life, every day, and still not understanding how this could possibly be the case helps me understand the stigma around mental health. The one thing I hate about writing is that it alters time so much. It condenses things that take time and expands things that don't. Some things take a long while to change. Other things change so quickly that you can't understand what's happening. I have tried to put five thousand days of my life into this book, and I can guarantee that stuff changed on every one of those days. Some battles take a long time to beat. I don't think I've won yet. I don't think the battle will ever be completely over. I'm telling you this because sometimes when I read stories about people, and it seems like they are able to change so quickly. I get mad at myself for taking such a long time. I want you to know that it does take a long time. No matter what it may seem like. We are all real people, and shit happens.

There is a wonderful intelligence to the unconscious, not because it's always smarter than we are, but because it's always more powerful than we are. We see things on the news about how this person killed himself, and this person brought a gun to school and threatened to kill this person. I used to not be able to understand how this person could think about doing some of these things. I hear people ask, "What must have been going through his mind for him to try to do that?" Only recently have I understood, and I don't think I like understanding it. I hope that people don't have to understand, but sometimes feeling your *it* helps to put everything in perspective.

While I truly believe, "We can't choose where we come from, but we can choose where we go," there is still some part of me that thinks there is only so much we can choose. I say to myself that I'm going to do this or that today, choosing something that I've never done before, but it usually ends up with me not being able to do it. I know that, in time, this will come and that out of one hundred days of not being able to do something, there will be one day that I can. It is not a zero-sum game.

And I know that when I was in elementary school, there were thousands of times that I *couldn't* do something. In kindergarten, if you told me I would be able to one day stand up in front of the class and give a presentation, I would never have believed it in a million years.

This other part of me that I feel bad talking about is that I'm angry at myself for not "choosing where I go from there" enough times. I let *it* take over too much. Just this year was the first time I ever went somewhere with someone from school. And the first time since kindergarten that I went over to someone's house. I've never been out with my friends late at night or been to a party. I've never had a date or a girlfriend. It's a lot to be mad at myself for missing, and I don't like thinking about it because it makes me angry. I will never be able to relive those moments or get any of them back to try again. They will only be memories that I can't change. I won't be the kid who gets to read this so he can understand that it's important to live now, to make the most of it, to not let *it* get in the way, no matter how much smarter *it* thinks it is.

Now, the other part of me wants to forget about all of this, because there is no way to change the past. The only thing for me to do is to let it go and move on because the more I think about it, the madder I get.

It was just like how I went from my middle school to MDS. No one knew the old me; no one knew me as the kid who didn't talk. I got the chance to remake myself, but I didn't. Four years later, they still see me as the quiet kid who keeps to himself and doesn't do much. Now when I go to college, I can remake myself to the person I've become. I think about how quickly things seemed to change from not really having any friends or having a feeling of not belonging somewhere to how I feel today, when every day I can't wait to go back to school to see the people who make me feel like I belong somewhere.

Then I think about how quickly things are going to change back when I go to college and that I won't know anyone. And it makes me angry to think that I only have a month of this feeling left and that I could have had it before, if I were different. But I am the way I am, and I have to deal with it. And the reality is that these people aren't disappearing. I'm just scared to think that I might snap when high school ends and I'm stuck in the same place I was before. I don't know what college will be like or how I'll react. I know *it* will be there, but I don't know how often or if I'll be strong enough to push back.

Please believe me when I tell you not to think of this as a sad story. I don't want you to feel bad. I just want you to think. I don't believe there are any sad stories, just life stories. They're all stories that make us appreciate the wonders of life and the randomness and happenstance of it all. If you were to take away one of the dominos, the rest don't fall the same way or land on the same path. You get to place your next domino. Just watch it fall and lead to the next one when it happens.

Recovery
By a friend

To the ones that had hope,
To the ones that saw more,
To the ones that never gave up on me,
Thank you.

Thank you for your support and your patience.
Thank you for your ears, your eyes, and your heart.

It's been a long time coming,
And a long winding road.
There's been bumps, ups and downs,
And many misleading forks.

But I can sincerely say that I'm the better,
For coming out of that dark tunnel,
And finally seeing the light.

What makes me strong is admitting my weakness,
What makes me love is remembering the hurt.

There are no excuses in life,
But you can be forgiven if you accept responsibility for your actions.

Beware of your thoughts because they become your actions,
Be wary of your actions because they turn into your habits,
Your habits then form your character,
And your character, your destiny.

There is no crime in peace of mind,
And no guilt in tenderness of display.
Great men can also be good men,
And the stars do not write the tales of our lives.

For this I know now.

And for this, I have found what has been missing,
Relocated what has been replaced,
Glimpsed truth,
And discovered contentedness.

The first step to recovery is admitting misstep.
So let us begin again,
Forge this tail anew,
And uncover what has long been hidden.

To at long last, but not finally, recover.

About the Author

Jonathan Kohlmeier was diagnosed with Selective Mutism when he was 5 years old and Social Anxiety soon after. He completed his memoir about his journey at the age of 19 and is passionate about confronting the stigma of mental health issues in society.